About the authors

Malcolm MacLachlan is with the Centre for Global Health and the School of Psychology at Trinity College Dublin, Ireland, and is currently a visiting professor at the Centre for Rehabilitation Studies, Stellenbosch University, South Africa and at the Department of Global Health and Social Medicine, Harvard University. Mac has worked as a clinician, consultant and academic, and has lived in Ireland, the UK, Malawi and South Africa. His interests are in promoting inclusive global health – especially regarding disability and ethnicity – and humanitarian work psychology. He has worked with a broad range of government and civil society organizations and multilateral agencies (including WHO, Unicef, UNHCR, OECD and UNESCO). He is the director of the International Doctoral School for Global Health (Indigo).

Stuart C. Carr is professor of psychology at the Industrial and Organizational (I/O) Psychology Programme, Massey University, New Zealand. He coordinates the Poverty Research Group, an international network focused on interdisciplinary approaches to reducing poverty. He also co-convenes the Global Task Force on Humanitarian Work Psychology. He was the lead investigator on Project ADDUP, a multi-country DFID/ESRC-funded study of pay and remuneration diversity in developing economies. Stuart has worked and lived in the UK, Malawi, remote Australia, Indonesia, Thailand, and New Zealand/Aotearoa. His books are among the first to examine poverty reduction from an I/O, work psychology perspective. Stuart has liaised extensively with for- and not-for-profit organizations. He co-edits the *Journal of Pacific Rim Psychology*, which has a focus on development.

Eilish McAuliffe is director of the Centre for Global Health at Trinity College Dublin, Ireland. She has worked as a clinician, consultant and academic and lived in Ireland, the UK, South Africa and Malawi, where she worked for Unicef and Irish Aid. Her research is on strengthening health systems in middle- and low-income countries, with a particular focus on the human resource crisis and maternal healthcare. In Ireland, she has also researched strategy and organizational change, and user involvement in health planning. Eilish has provided a wide range of consultancy support to governments, NGOs and professional healthcare bodies and has contributed to numerous strategy and policy documents in healthcare in both high- and low-income countries.

Praise for *The Aid Triangle*

'MacLachlan, Carr and McAuliffe have used sound social and behavioural science concepts and empirical evidence to challenge the very notion of international aid. Using the core principles of dominance, injustice and threats to cultural identity, they identify what is basically ineffective, and even counterproductive, in the current system of international aid and development. This book is a most welcome addition to the growing call to rethink this whole dimension of international relations.' *John Berry, professor emeritus, Queen's University, Canada*

'This approachable and imaginative book takes a very different look at the practice of international aid. Written by social scientists with considerable experience in the area, it offers not only a critique of current practices but also advice about how really to help those who need it. It is written with passion and clarity but always supported by the scientific literature in the area. It deserves to be, and I am sure will be, read by many working in international aid worldwide.' *Professor Adrian Furnham, University College London*

'At last! A book that addresses the psychological politics braided through civil society, governmental and multilateral agencies involved in aid. Confronting the taboos of implicit dominance and its associated injustices, this book argues for the importance of strengthening local capabilities and identities, particularly among those traditionally marginalized by mainstream society. I highly recommend it.' *A. K. Dube, CEO, Secretariat of the African Decade for Persons with Disability, South Africa*

'*The Aid Triangle* is a thought-provoking book that poses key questions about the nature and mechanisms of development. It is an anthropocentric and humane analysis of the contemporary industry of international relations, striving with humility for both the giver and receiver of aid to "develop" through creative action. The book identifies the human at the centre of international assistance as the origin of an appropriate hermeneutic of development, but cogently argues that recognition of this human concern is generally "taboo", trumped by the interests of business and politics. Taking cues from social-psychological evaluation of the nature of giving, the authors challenge the neoliberal priorities of modern development practice, and envision an approach to international assistance free from dominance, injustice and the suppression of local identity.' *Professor Alastair Ager, executive director, Global Health Initiative, Mailman School of Public Health, Columbia University, USA*

'This book places justice – between individuals, between organizations and between countries and international organisations – at the heart of international aid and development, explaining its relationship with dominance and identity in a challenging, authoritative and engaging way.' *Mary Robinson, founder and chair, Realizing Rights: The Ethical Globalization Initiative*

To the many friends and colleagues
whom we have lost to HIV/AIDS

THE AID TRIANGLE
recognizing the human dynamics of dominance, justice and identity

Malcolm MacLachlan, Stuart C. Carr
and Eilish McAuliffe

Fernwood Publishing
HALIFAX | WINNIPEG

Zed Books
LONDON · NEW YORK

The Aid Triangle: Recognizing the human dynamics of dominance, justice and identity was first published in 2010

Published in Canada by Fernwood Publishing Ltd, 32 Oceanvista Lane, Black Point, Nova Scotia BOJ 1BO
<www.fernwoodpublishing.ca>

Published in the rest of the world by Zed Books Ltd, 7 Cynthia Street, London N1 9JF, UK and Room 400, 175 Fifth Avenue, New York, NY 10010, USA

www.zedbooks.co.uk

Copyright © Malcolm MacLachlan, Stuart C. Carr, Eilish McAuliffe 2010

The rights of Malcolm MacLachlan, Stuart C. Carr and Eilish McAuliffe to be identified as the authors of this work have been asserted by them in accordance with the Copyright, Designs and Patents Act, 1988

Set in Monotype Sabon and Gill Sans Heavy by Ewan Smith, London
Index ed.emery@thefreeuniversity.net
Cover designed by Rogue Four Design
Printed and bound in Great Britain by CPI Antony Rowe, Chippenham and Eastbourne

Distributed in the USA exclusively by Palgrave Macmillan, a division of St Martin's Press, LLC, 175 Fifth Avenue, New York, NY 10010, USA

A catalogue record for this book is available from the British Library
Library of Congress Cataloging in Publication Data available

Library and Archives Canada Cataloguing in Publication
MacLachlan, Malcolm
    The aid triangle : recognising the human dynamics of dominance, justice and identity / Malcolm Maclachlan, Eilish McAuliffe, Stuart C. Carr.
Co-published by Zed Books.
Includes bibliographical references and index.
ISBN 978-1-55266-370-7
    1. Economic assistance--Developing countries. 2. Economic development--Developing countries. 3. Dominance (Psychology). 4. Social justice. 5. National characteristics. I. Mc Auliffe, Eilish II. Carr, Stuart C. III. Title.
HC60.M33 2010   338.9009172'4   C2010-901866-4

ISBN 978 1 84277 910 1 hb (Zed Books)
ISBN 978 1 84277 911 8 pb (Zed Books)
ISBN 978 1 84277 835 3 eb (Zed Books)
ISBN 978 1 55266 370 7 (Fernwood Publishing)

Contents

Tables, figures and boxes | viii
Acknowledgements | ix

1 Introduction 1

2 Aid 10

3 Dominance 23

4 Justice 59

5 Identity 80

6 Learning 119

7 Conclusion 141

Bibliography | 154
Index | 167

Tables, figures and boxes

Tables

2.1 Some emphatic and emotive book titles attesting to
problems in international aid 11

3.1 Planning balance sheet for project aid and direct budget
support 31

3.2 Causes associated with most popular celebrities 42

4.1 A taxonomy of work justice. 62

4.2 Items on which pay groups differed. 73

6.1 A taxonomy of organizational learning 125

6.2 Principles to facilitate learning in partnerships 130

Figures

1.1 The aid triangle. 7

3.1 An inverse resonance effect in Tanzania 46

3.2 Perceived social dominance in different countries 49

4.1 Relationship between job satisfaction and managerial
consideration. .67

4.2 Degree of job satisfaction related to satisfaction with
different aspects of the job 68

4.3 Theoretical coping strategies in aid projects 71

5.1 Navigating the dynamics of aid and development 89

Boxes

1.1 Oxfamming the world 1

1.2 Philanthropy vs the generosity of the taxpayer 2

3.1 Some thoughts on celebrity and international aid 40

4.1 Indicative quotes from qualitative research in the Solomon
Islands 75

6.1 Reported Irish NGO activity in Africa, circa 2005. . . . 132

Acknowledgements

This book has grown out of our collective work on international aid and 'development' over the past twenty years. Our 'collective' is much broader and greater than just the three of us, and so we owe a debt of sincere gratitude to the very many students, practitioners, funders, civil servants, government ministers, aid agency employees, and others, who have helped to shape our thinking and helped us to be more critical of, and reflexive about, our own research and practice.

We also wish to express our gratitude to organizations that have supported our work in recent years: these include, in Ireland, Irish Aid, Irish Research Council for the Humanities and Social Sciences, Enterprise Ireland, Health Research Board and Higher Education Authority; in the UK, the Department for International Development and the Economic and Social Research Council; in New Zealand, NZAID and in Australia AusAID; in South Africa, the National Research Foundation; and internationally, the World Bank, World Health Organization and the European Union Framework Programme.

We are grateful to the team at Zed Books for their prompt and professional processing of our manuscript.

1 | Introduction

1 Oxfamming the world

Binyavanga Wainaina's 'Continental Drift' column in the *Mail & Guardian* (South Africa) of 30 November 2007 presented an angry and sarcastic image of aid that people in the donor countries rarely see:

Hello kitty kitty kitty ... Are you an orphan? Are you Sudanese? Chadian? Are you sub-Saharan African suffering from mild mental retardation? Are you an African woman suffering from the African male? Would you like an Oxfam biscuit? Organic anti-retrovirals? Have you been raped? You might not know it, but you are an orphan, a refugee. Can we fly 103 of you to France to be loved? We can breastfeed you. We can make you a Darfur orphan. Even if you are not. If you are black and under 10 years old, please come and talk to us.

Come kitty kitty.

We can save you from yourself. We can save ourselves from our terrible selves. Help us to Oxfam the whole black world, to make it a better place. ...

Instead of sweatshops, we will have Ubuntu shops where you can arrive in biodegradable loincloths to make bone jewellery for caring people who earn $1 million a year, live in San Francisco or Cape Town and feel bad about this. In our future world you will have three balanced meals a day.

In the afternoons Jeffrey Sachs will come and show the boys how to build a gender-friendly communal anti-poverty village where all base human emotions – lust, greed and competition – will be sustainably developed out of your heads, along with truly dangerous ideas such as rebellion. After playing non-violent games (rope skipping and hugging), you will write letters to your loving step-parent in Toronto. For an hour a day we will teach you how to make clothes, shelter and shoes out of recycled bottle tops in Ndebele colours. ...

Trust us. You can't do it yourselves. We have dedicated our lives to you. Come kitties, come to mummy (p. 32).

2 Philanthropy vs the generosity of the taxpayer

A letter in the Christmas edition of the *Irish Times*, 2007, presented a somewhat cynical impression, not so much of the gift-giving of the 'The Great and the Good', but of their eulogizing in comparison to the 42 per cent tax 'generosity' of the average Irish taxpayer:

Madam,

No doubt JP McManus deserves the award of Philanthropist of the Year and Niall Mellon is a worthy recipient of International Philanthropist of the Year. Sir Anthony O'Reilly basks in the warm glow of his altruism. Bono and Bob Geldof are fêted and renowned for their efforts at eliminating global poverty.

However, as a lowly taxpayer I and others like me have few opportunities to don a tuxedo or affect a carefully cultivated 'scruffy look'. Meanwhile every Euro in income tax paid by me and the rest of the State's resident workforce disappears into health and other state services to little acclaim.

I am not at all envious of those whose huge wealth requires that they live in offshore tax havens or who are able to structure their wealth in tax-efficient vehicles. I fully accept that the taxation system be used to fuel an entrepreneurial culture. However, I find it increasingly nauseating to have to endure the fawning and sycophantic eulogies delivered on those who are fortunate enough to select pet projects for their patronage.

I have no choice about where my money is spent. ... I too could manage a wry knowing smile as my generosity was fêted and my modesty would be evident in my thank you speech. Perhaps the Revenue Commissioners might institute the inaugural awards ceremony for Taxpayer of the Year, 2008 (Michael J. Shovelin, Sligo, p. 17).

This book is about the human dynamics of international aid. We illustrate how the aid system incorporates power relationships, and therefore relationships of *dominance*. We explore how such dominance can be both a cause and a consequence of *injustice*. We explain how the experience of injustice is both a challenge and a stimulus to personal, community and national *identity*, and how such identities underlie the human potential that international aid should seek to enrich. We argue that these three concepts can provide a framework that can be used to triangulate and improve our understanding of why aid sometimes works and sometimes doesn't, and more importantly how to make it work better.

Using the concepts of dominance, justice and identity, *The Aid Triangle* seeks to provide a framework for producing more empowering and more effective aid, based on an understanding of the human dynamics through which all aid must flow. We consider how people take actions which strive to maintain or achieve identity, esteem and empowerment, and how aid efforts and development work may present obstacles to this because, ironically, the human dynamics and symbolism embedded in the processes of development work often challenge rather than promote individuals' and communities' sense of identity. We consider the psychology behind the political reality of international aid and the dynamics that are common to relationships at all levels of the aid system.

This book thus seeks a new paradigm for aid, by thinking it through, in Schumacher's words, 'as if people mattered'. Aid is an emotive subject, both from the supplier's and the receiver's side, as is illustrated in the examples above. It resonates powerfully with ideas of justice and identity, and the nature of relationships between people. The book has been written at a time when the global economy and global society are being forced to recognize the unfortunate consequences of unregulated and often unrestrained greed. We are cognizant that the interconnections between domnance, injustice and identity are perhaps relevant to a much wider arc of human activity than international aid. Let us first, though, explore briefly the concept of development.

The idea of development

Just what is it that international aid is supposed to be aiding? Ideally, it is the poorest of the poor; ideally, it is a process that empowers and enables the poor to take concrete steps to stay alive and to improve the quality and length of their lives. But what do we call that? It's not economic growth; that may be part of the process that achieves it, but it should not, in its own right, be a goal (as we argue later). People often call both the process and the outcome of the process of things getting better in poor countries 'development'. The term in itself is not problematic, but the uses it is put to are. For instance, the aid community talk about 'least developed countries', 'developing countries' and 'developed countries'. It is generally felt in the aid industry that people who are pedantic about the use of such terms are a bit of a pain in the arse! That everybody knows their limitations, but 'ah, sure, we'll use them anyway, and we don't mean any harm by them'.

Regardless of such thoughtless good intentions, what happens is that ideas of the extent of development start to frame how people see each other, and therefore how they behave towards each other. In some of the poorer countries where we have worked there is often semantic confusion between the terms 'expert' and 'expat' (as in expatriate worker – a person coming from outside the country in question), which sometimes are taken to be literally synonymous, causing bafflement at the idea of having two words for the same thing! On the side of the international development workers, the idea of 'me developed, you still developing' gets confused with ideas about the rate of economic growth, foreign direct investment, gross domestic product and so on, such that indices of these are actually taken to be indicators of the 'state of development', conveniently summarizing a country's diversity of needs – including diversity in income – in a few banal clinical statistics. Worse still, some associate differing degrees of development with differing levels of intellectual and cultural sophistication. Cultures thousands of years old are seen as primitive and their adherents as in need of 'development'. These connotations are often not implicit and indeed often not intended, but they do nonetheless pattern thinking about development and personify the sort of implicit superiority that has led to the many effects of social dominance of one group by another, which we will be considering in Chapter 3.

The word 'development' doesn't, however, work well even for those of us in rich countries. If we have reached an end stage in the process of developing and are now 'developed', what do we call it when things get better? For instance, from the mid-1990s to the mid-2000s, things in Ireland changed utterly, with staggering rates of 'Celtic Tiger' economic growth, unprecedented rates of worker immigration, and dramatically increased incomes. Was that development? If it happened in Papua New Guinea, would that be development? If it was development in Ireland, then does that mean the Irish weren't developed in the early 1990s? And what of the downturn/credit crunch/correction/recession? Are we now 'un-developing'?

Clearly all countries have the potential for things to change and for the lives of people in them to improve, and in that sense all countries should strive to be developing countries, and all politicians should be delighted when their party is seen to be running a developing country. In fact, they should feel rather awkward when asked what their government is doing for 'developing countries', as that would imply their own country isn't developing. Our point is that when words are used carelessly, they can construct a web of meanings that may be quite unintended, but nonetheless detrimental to others; even those whom we consciously wish to 'aid'.

In this book we will use the term 'low-income country' to refer to that group of countries you may think of as 'developing countries'. Of course, 'low-income country' is not ideal either, as it implies that the income of a country is its most important descriptor, ignores the fact that average income can hide huge inequalities and perhaps implies that assistance should be targeted at increasing incomes, rather than improving human rights, access to health services or educational provision. However, to ignore the scale of the differences in average monthly income for, say, a bus driver in Germany (the equivalent of US$2,156) and one in Peru (the equivalent of US$140 – see www.worldsalaries.org/busdriver.shtml) would not be helpful. Whatever term is used to refer to those countries that fail to adequately provide the human rights, well-being and opportunities that their citizens are entitled to strive for, that term will be only partially adequate because of the interlocking and multifarious nature of people's lives. In using the term 'low-income countries' we hope to reduce the negative connotations and implication of inferiority associated with those who are not from financially better-off countries. If you feel that the polar opposite of our term – that is, 'high-income countries' – implies superiority, then we would disagree. Occasionally in this book we will lapse back into the 'developed–developing' jargon, either in quoting others or to make a point, particularly in regard to the idea of the social dominance of one group over others, and the many undesirable consequences of it for improving the lives of the poorest people.

Relational development

We did say there was nothing wrong with the term 'development' per se, but the idea of 'development' should now be understood to be about groups of people in *reciprocal relationships* that represent improving circumstances for all involved. It is not something that one country *does* to or for another; it is something they help each other with. While such development may have reciprocal economic benefits, such as opening new opportunities for (Fair) trade, it is increasingly being understood to be inescapably embedded in other factors too. For instance, development must concern the effects of one country's activities on the worldwide physical environment, shared by all. Development must consider how supporting certain types of political systems over others is likely to affect the world-wide security environment shared by all, with increasing democracy hopefully promoting greater security by giving marginalized groups a greater voice. The deliberate underproduction of trained health-care professionals in high-income countries, with the intention of poaching these from low-income countries, is not 'development' for either of them; it suggests an uneven division of responsibility and lack of commitment to global health on the part of rich countries (McAuliffe and MacLachlan 2005).

Development is what happens when relationships strengthen for the common good; it has a moral dimension and can best be achieved by processes that are emancipatory – where what is being done in the name of 'development' contributes to achieving its aims. This means putting people first, or, as the *Report of the South Commission* put it, as long ago as 1990: 'Development has therefore to be an effort of, by and for the people. True development has to be *people-centred*' (emphasis added). When countries, organizations, groups or individuals are involved in 'development', they are in relationships that eschew dominance, promote justice and support positive identities.

A systems triangle

We argue that dominance, justice and identity are critical themes running through international aid and development, and that their influence has not been sufficiently recognized or understood. For instance, Forsyth's otherwise excellent and comprehensive *Encyclopaedia of International Development*, published in 2005, does not contain entries for any of our three terms; yet we believe these concepts are omnipresent, although often implicit and even taboo, in much aid work. Understanding how the three dynamics, dominance, justice and identity, interact and shape the relationships of aid is a first step to improving the processes and hopefully the effectiveness of aid and development. We are not interested in building a 'grand theory' of development, but rather a simple understanding

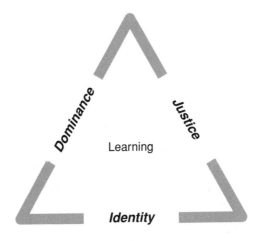

FIGURE I.I The aid triangle

(by 'simple', we of course don't mean 'simplistic', we mean easy to make useful) that stops people in their tracks long enough for them to learn that there is an alternative to slotting into the same unthinking, repetitive groove that has characterized much of the ineffective aid work that we are all too aware of.

The triangular relationship shown in Figure 1.1 presents us with a challenge in writing this book. The three core concepts interact in a dynamic way within aid relationships, making it difficult to separate and discuss each independently. We could try to show the three elements at work in a variety of situations, or we could try to show the relevance of each of the three concepts, and then show how their interrelationship can help us improve the effectiveness of aid. We have chosen the latter option. Following a review of aid in Chapter 2, the next three chapters address dominance, justice and identity in turn. Because of the dynamic relationships at play this is an artificial separation, and we have accepted in the writing of this book the inevitable overlap that occurs in outlining the interconnectivity between our three core elements. The sort of systems thinking, the interlocking nature of human dynamics, that we want to encourage is a feature of the book, and so you will find reference to justice, for example, not only in Chapter 4 but in all chapters. We hope that this deliberate cross-hatching will enrich, rather than detract from, our readers' understanding of the aid triangle.

Our approach

In this book we have sought to focus on the human dynamics of everyday social life in aid and 'development' organizations, and we are aware that we have done this quite selectively. We have not, for instance, considered the excellent work done by the Antares Foundation, People in Aid, the Huntington Institute, or many others, in helping aid workers manage the stress of their work, and their own health and welfare. These constitute perhaps the more 'obvious' and public face of the tremendous difficulties encountered in working in this field.

Yet we are very aware that these issues interact with and are perhaps sometimes symptomatic of concerns about dominance, justice and identity. As such, we have chosen to focus more on the background, and often implicit, factors, and less on the foreground, and explicit, concerns that people struggle with. We hope that in doing so we have nonetheless been able to illustrate how real, immediate and tangible the aid triangle is.

2 | Aid

'Defence of liberty which is allied with defence of privileged status is fairly suspect' René Dumont, 1966

'… the numbers of poor people in whose name development is justified are greater than they were when it was invented, and in many cases their poverty stems directly from the havoc it has wreaked on their lives. Under these circumstances, is the concept any longer useful?' Black (2002: 10)

'One of the most depressing aspects of the whole aid fiasco is that donors, policymakers, governments, academicians, economists and development specialists know, in their heart of hearts, that aid doesn't work, hasn't worked and won't work' Moyo (2009: 46)

The idea of aid

Why is helping people so difficult? You have something, you give it to someone who needs it; you feel good, they are better off and possibly more able to help themselves in future. That's the basic idea of international aid. In economics, the idea that anything that makes one person or group better off without making the other any worse off is called a 'Pareto improvement/efficiency' (after the economist Pareto). Sometimes aid works, and works well. Recently, however, alongside the increase in resources being made available for international aid, there is also increasing awareness of the challenges it faces. Hang on, that's a euphemism; not 'challenges', massive problems! Many commentators – for instance, Sen (2000), Sachs (2005), Collier (2007) and Moyo (2009) – are calling for a rethink of what international aid is and how it's done. Table 2.1, which catalogues some of the 'catchier' titles of books in this area, surely intimates that something is amiss, and has been for quite some time.

TABLE 2.1 Some emphatic and emotive book titles attesting to problems in international aid

---

Dead Aid: Why aid is not working and how there is another way for Africa, Damisa Moyo

Lords of Poverty: The power, prestige, and corruption of the international aid business, Graham Hancock

The Road to Hell: The ravaging effects of foreign aid and international charity, Michael Maren

The Trouble with Africa: Why foreign aid isn't working, Robert Calderisi

Pathologies of Power: Health, human rights, and the new war on the poor, Paul Farmer

Dying for Growth: Global inequality and the health of the poor, Jim Yong Kim and Joyce Millen

The White Man's Burden: Why the West's efforts to aid the rest have done so much ill and so little good, William Easterly

---

In this book we want to offer some new ways of thinking about what aid is, and how it can be done better. Our basic idea is that it is people who make aid work, not money, technology or expertise; not information systems or fancy new buildings; not business-class flights or air-conditioned four-wheel-drive vehicles. As Black also argues, 'some type of gadget, medicine, or piece of kit may have widespread application. But true development is about people, and social beings do not function mechanically' (2002: 9); to paraphrase, 'it's the people, stupid'. If the very system of international aid creates relationships between people that perpetuate the inequalities it is actually meant to address, then 'trying to help' does harm. It maintains poverty, heightens frustration, promotes arrogance, rationalizes disengagement, alienates the disempowered and silences the voiceless. We do not suggest that the perspective we offer here is complete. But we do argue that no other perspective is complete without it.

This chapter briefly considers the relationship between aid and development over the past fifty years. Its focus is on the sort of relationships that have been cultivated between people in different parts of the world, and between different people engaged in aid and 'development' projects in the same part of the world. We believe that there are three crucial themes that flow like underground streams through the international aid landscape, bubbling to the surface in some places, seeping into the sand in others and spouting into the air in well-publicized aid crises every now and again. These three themes, however, don't traverse aid-land in nice straight lines that are easy to divine. We consider these themes one at a time. The themes of *dominance, justice* and *identity* are developed in Chapters 3, 4 and 5. They don't jump out at everyday observers of aid; they are often subterranean, meandering through human misery, flowing into each other, creating eddies, whirlpools and the odd Jacuzzi! After considering how these ideas apply to aid, Chapter 6 asks, 'What needs to happen so that we are not condemned to repeat our mistakes? How can we learn better from our successes and failures?' Chapter 7 integrates our conclusions.

Social dominance occurs where some groups in society assume a superior role to other groups. Such relationships are common in the myriad international aid hierarchies, and their consequences pattern interactions at personal, group, institutional and international levels. The sense of implicit social dominance in international aid taints people's experience of what is just and fair, which is quite ironic, given that aid is often directed at redressing situations of injustice, inequity and oppression. When an individual's or a group's sense of justice is threatened, so is the basis on which they derive these values: their identity. When identity is challenged it can sometimes give rise to very positive behaviours, but also, at times, to defensive, destructively competitive and overly assertive behaviours, which we also know can characterize aid.

We are starting to emerge from a primarily economics-driven 'black box' mentality regarding development: money in, a certain level of production or service out, and bemusement at what went on in between! Here, we step into the black box and find that people's lives and the meanings they construct are not passively received, handed out or carelessly stumbled upon. They are actively maintained by individuals and communities striving to make sense of what are often quite desperate situations with apparently bizarrely motivated interventions by 'aidies'. In wanting aid to 'work' for most people, in most places, most of the time, we understand that there are some commonalities that may be generalized across many contexts, but there will also be particular situations, stretching beyond the scope of such commonalities.

We also recognize that international aid occurs in a very broad social, political and economic context, and that these relations are to some extent indivisible. We don't seek to divide them; rather we seek to consider the human dynamics through which they operate. *Homo economicus* needs not only to be sniffing around in the detail of Poverty Reduction Strategy Papers (PRSPs), project management and sector-wide plans, but also to stand up and look *Homo erectus* in the eye, to see what's really going on between the people 'doing' and the people 'receiving' aid.

Let's take an example, and one from our own backyard; in fact from an organization for which we have a great deal of respect and commitment. What we are about to say applies to many such organizations, and we have made up a rather nondescript name to emphasize that point. The World Improvement Alliance (WIA) sought to provide a voice and a mechanism for researchers from low-income countries to come together with global policy-makers from multilateral agencies and representatives from (rich) country aid programmes. WIA's annual conference is a great idea. The conference is dominated by neoliberalists, who quite cleverly have produced their own little neoliberal intellectual market by awarding prizes to the 'best' (generally neoliberal) research from those 'developing countries'. The guys from the 'developed countries' – let's call them the 'developed guys' – give awards to the guys from the 'developing countries' – let's call them the 'underdeveloped guys'. The 'developed guys' are frequently Ivy League professors, and the 'underdeveloped guys' are frequently graduates from US or European top-notch universities. Sometimes, but not often enough, 'really underdeveloped guys' who are graduates from universities in the 'really undeveloped countries' actually get the prize. In doing so they help WIA to fulfil its mission; a worthy mission, to which many excellent and genuine people are strongly committed.

The mood music is all wrong, however; the process is one of affirmation by established elites, of reward for coming up to 'their standard'. We could have picked on any number of development networks or conferences. We picked on WIA, because we are part of it and because we know there are loads of people in it who are seriously dedicated to achieving its goals. Like so much else in development work, how we go about it often undermines what we want to achieve. The symbolism – which the main actors may sublimate – works against the idea, and when symbolism is more vivid than ideas, things can go awry.

It is up to all of us who value the goals of any WIA-type organization to create a process that is part of the desired outcome. It would be nice, for instance, if a panel of civil servants from low-income countries sat in judgment of how useful the research output from different research groups was, and what efforts these groups have made to promote its utilization. Of course, some kind of legitimation of dissent, to challenge the power-brokered system itself, might have to be ensured beforehand.

While such conferences can of course just be a talking shop, they can also be important windows into other people's minds, if not souls. In 2008, Nobel Prize-winning economist Michael Spence, in a keynote address at the Global Development Network's annual conference, reminded the audience – primarily made up of economists – that it is not economic growth that we should be interested in, but rather what economic growth can potentially deliver. Sometimes, however – indeed, in each of the ten 'top growth' countries that he discussed – economic growth increased income inequality; presumably with the poorest and most needy reaping the least benefit. Even when economies do grow well, the allocation of benefits can leave the majority disenchanted, as was clearly demonstrated by the voting out of an Indian government that had produced very impressive economic growth. Thus how growth happens, and not just growth itself, is of critical importance.

Michael Spence also highlighted that one of the most important drivers of economic growth is the health of the population, in particular its nutritional status. For Spence, one of the valued outcomes of growth is, in fact, improved health. If health is both a key driver of economic growth and one of its major benefits, then, we might ask, why not invest primarily in health rather than in the economy? Why not get into a virtuous cycle of health improvement, a by-product of which would be economic growth? When one of us asked, given the scenario just described, 'How would you divide up $100 between a ministry of health and a ministry of economic development in a low-income country?', Michael dithered. Being a smart guy, he suggested that how much the respective ministries already had would have to be taken into account, but being a good sport, and entering into the spirit of the (serious) jibe, he did entertain the possibility of giving more money to the ministry of health. His fellow keynote speaker on the opening day, Graeme Wheeler, managing director (operations), World Bank, was more forthcoming, however, suggesting that, indeed, the greater part of the $100 would have to be spent on health. Neither, of course, revealed just how much; they are economists, after all!

Recently we were invited to run a workshop on interdisciplinary research for development for the Global Development Network. Increasingly it is being recognized that the over-identification of 'development' with the (necessarily) narrow views of one discipline is not helpful. Trying to put the development camel through the eye of an economist's needle is a difficult trick. Economics is, of course, a vital element of understanding human behaviour as it relates to economic development, but by itself is necessarily insufficient. The problem is that most economists have been socialized into a professional environment where this is not understood. Even when embracing the idea of interdisciplinarity, some may continue to feel that economics, for most 'development' issues, will remain the 'core discipline' (see Gobind Nankani's foreword on interdisciplinary research for development in MacLachlan, Carr and McWha 2008).

Resistance to insensitive macroeconomics for 'developing countries' has come from many places, including, it has to be said, economists themselves. Schumacher asked us to think that 'Small is Beautiful', and poignantly subtitled his classic 'Economics as if people mattered'. So while Bill Clinton judged that it was the 'economy, stupid' that got him elected, and Simon Maxwell, director of the Overseas Development Institute, told us 'it's the economy stupid' (2004) when it comes to international development, given what Michael Spence and many others have realized, it's not the economy, *it's the people*, and they ain't stupid! If development is for the people, then it has to be about the people. Models of economic development that see the betterment of the poorest of the poor as a way-downstream consequence of economic growth are just not good enough. While accepting the systems-based thinking of macroeconomics, we do not accept the idea of intervening in the system upstream, where the rich folk live. Surely the whole point of a systems-based analysis is that you can intervene anywhere in a series of linked-up processes, and it will have knock-on effects. Why not intervene where you most want those effects? The grounding of development initiatives in the lives of the poor should be the starting point, and this has also been recognized by some of the most remarkable economists of our time, such as Amartya Sen (1999, 2009), Grameen Bank founder Muhammad Yunus (both Nobel laureates) and Building Resources Across Communities (BRAC) founder and chairperson Fazle Hasan Abed (surely deserving of same). In Chapter 7 we consider their work further, and the idea that the process of development should be emancipating; as Gandhi said, we 'must be the change we seek'. For now we briefly reflect on some of the history that is pertinent to our argument and that has led to the current state of 'our development'.

The political economy of aid

Leopold Senghor observed in the early 1960s (Balandier, pp. 264–5, in G. Arnold 2005: 57) that: 'What all these distinguished minds want, whether they are Westerners or Easterners, is to superimpose a European civilisation upon us, to impregnate us with it in the name of universality. Hence exotic peoples such as ourselves would be eternally condemned to be not the producers but the consumers of civilisations.'

This is nowhere more starkly demonstrated – in the nineties and possibly still – than when the French Department at the University of Malawi's Chancellor College taught a course simply entitled 'Civilization'. When a member of the department was asked by one of us whether they would consider qualifying the name of the course by inserting the word 'French' at the beginning, we were met with quizzical disdain! Ronald Segal, writing in 1966, suggested that the West's attitudes to the newly independent African countries was that the rejection of the former colonial ruler's 'standards, its institutions, its continuing supervision is not just stupidity, it is ingratitude' (p. 104).

Perhaps the Europeans of the 1960s were still shackled to the atavistic attitudes of the slave trade and other facets of colonial exploitation and savagery, for in 1960 the African continent's population, having been equivalent to that of Europe's in the eighteenth century, had been reduced to only one twelfth of Europe's population in the 1960s (Arnold 2005). Arnold also notes that, prior to independence, the African student returning from academic success abroad found that he was downgraded and paid less at home than his white expatriate colleagues. 'The resulting bitterness rankled' (p. 68) back in the early 1960s, and fifty years later still does for contemporary graduates working alongside better-paid but similarly qualified 'aidies', or those in the commercial sector – an issue we will dissect in some detail later. Arnold also argues that when Africans did take over senior jobs, they wanted to retain the trappings of elitism that their predecessors had so carefully cultivated. The civil service embodied the Eurocentric class barriers, such as secluded housing, that were foreign to traditionally much more egalitarian societies. Those African countries that reached to the West also often sought to embody many of its status symbols.

In the 1960s many believed that aid could launch nation-states on to a trajectory of development, while African leaders frequently saw it as due recompense for the injustices of colonialism and as a balancing of budgets by loans and gifts from the 'mother countries' (Fanon 1965). A 'new class of modern empire builders' – the United Nations, the World Bank, national aid agencies and NGOs – proffered their expertise to 'guide the new states along development paths more in the interests of the external world from which they came than those of the new states' (Arnold 2005: 118). Arnold argues, persuasively, that even after the colonies become independent, the 'predominant western motive was to retain control over the levers of economic power' (p. 140). The need for this control was enhanced by the backdrop of the cold war, where the competition for influence, for bestowing favours on indebted dependants, for patronage, was intense, and where many countries felt they had to declare their colours for one bloc or the other in order to secure reliable commitment. As Rodney stated, most forcefully, in his *How Europe Underdeveloped Africa* (1972), however, the capitalist projects of the West never sought to develop capitalist rivals in Africa, but to continue to 'farm' it – the diamonds mined in Africa had the value added to them by their cutting in Europe, an exporting of and adding of value, only now being addressed in the new millennium by the opening of a diamond finishing facility in Gaborone.

Colonial economic growth had failed to produce an indigenous human infrastructure capable of taking over after independence – resulting in *dependence* being maintained to achieve the goals that had been swallowed by the new states. The paternalism and authoritarianism of the donors, and their demand for compliance with their own agendas, progressively broke the African spirit enlivened by the promise of autonomy that independence had implicitly given (Arnold 2005). It is staggering to think that on 30 October 1967 *The Times* (of London) argued thus:

> Unless something is done urgently to shock the donor countries out of their growing cynicism and prevarication, the 'have-nots' must inevitably lose patience and attempt to take the law into their own hands. A world so divided, not only economically, but also politically by a bottomless gulf of suspicion, incomprehension and bitterness, would be a world doomed to self-destruction. (Cited in ibid.: 151)

These attitudes, the cynicism, the lack of trust, the anger and frustration and bitterness of the 1960s, chartered the channels of a psychology (small 'p') of aid that continues to stain our current thinking (see, for instance, Moyo 2009).

When countries did produce the primary commodities that Western markets wanted, their gains were often offset by changing terms of trade, moving against the producers of primary commodities. These realities further spurred on an 'aid industry', which is defined by Arnold as 'the creation of structures to facilitate the provision of aid by the rich developed donor countries to the poor developing countries' (2005: 160). The OECD established its Development

Assistance Committee (DAC) and the United Nations proclaimed the 1960s 'the First Development Decade'; 'Aid had become an international fashion' (ibid.: 160), with former colonial powers (and others) establishing government departments or ministries of aid, or development, or cooperation, or whatever. Whether such government machinery was meant to serve as a conduit for recompense or to provide the levers for continuing economic control is ambiguous, but the need for such mechanisms to coincide with donors' political interests was no doubt as clear in the 1960s as it is today.

The new millennium

Along with a plethora of international initiatives, the Commission for Africa, a UK-based initiative, trumpeted new hope with the prospect of considerably more (new?) money to be given as aid. But here too the rhetoric is questionable. The Commission claims that: 'Africa is poor, ultimately, because its economy has not grown. The public and private sectors need to work together to create a climate which unleashes the entrepreneurship of the people of Africa, generates employment and encourages individuals and firms, domestic and foreign, to invest.'

Political scientist Patrick Bond from the University of Kwa Zulu Natal, however, rewrites it thus:

Africa is poor, ultimately, because the economy and society have been ravaged by international capital as well as by local elites who are often propped up by foreign powers. The public and private sectors have worked together to drain the continent of resources which otherwise – if harnessed and shared fairly – should meet the needs of the peoples of Africa. (Bond 2006: 1)

Even more emphatically, Bond argues that:

Thanks to politicians and bureaucrats in Washington and London, IMF and World Bank mandarins, Geneva trade hucksters, pliant NGOs, banal celebrities and the mass media, the legacy and ongoing exploitation of Africa have been ensnared in ideological confusion. (Ibid.: ix)

While much has been made of debt relief, it may be that much of what was relieved was never going to get paid in any case. The African Forum and Network on Debt and Development (AFRODAD) has argued that 'The relationship is still one of "if you want what we have to offer, you must do things our way"' (ibid.: 24). According to Bond, at the global level this still reflects well-entrenched power relations rather than anything that could be called 'participatory' (ibid.: 43). The power relationships between donor governments have also created difficulties with a pecking order of importance, often related to the size of the donor country's aid budget. Many of the global initiatives established in the past decade (e.g. the Global Fund to Fight HIV/AIDS, Tuberculosis and Malaria) have attempted to introduce more harmonization in aid. The recent announcement of President Obama's Global Health Initiative with an emphasis on partnering with other donor countries and working directly with the governments of recipient countries, also bodes well for more integrated approaches. One danger presented by these global efforts, however, is the exacerbation of the power imbalance between recipient country governments and these global partnerships with which they will have to negotiate for a sizeable portion of their budget. The potential for dominance is significantly greater. Black (2002) clearly expresses her frustration that 'Instead of creating a more equal world, five decades of "development" have produced a socio-economic global apartheid: small archipelagos of wealth, within and between nation states, surrounded by impoverished humanity' (ibid.: 13).

Perhaps anticipating the increase in aid funding subsequently announced by the G8, Black stressed that 'Although the quantity of ODA provided down the years remains an issue because it is so miserly, this is far less significant than issues associated with its quality and purpose' (ibid.: 30). Her reading of this is clearly one that chimes with our own concerns regarding dominance:

> ... aid created a new sub-set of international affairs, casting developed and developing countries respectively as 'donors' and 'recipients'. This relationship, in which the donors are in the driving seat, no matter how much this is glossed over with words such

as 'partnership', has helped to perpetuate an axis of superiority and inferiority. (Ibid.: 30–31)

While, of course, thinking has developed and practices have changed, it is also clear that international aid continues to be troubled by the nature of the 'giving' and 'receiving' relationships that it entails. Understanding the ramifications of such relationships is, we believe, at the root of providing more effective, more fruitful, international aid.

Inclusive development

If you are not so familiar with the world of international aid and development, it may seem odd that we feel the need to place special emphasis on poverty reduction among the poorest of the poor, or on the participation in society of those most marginalized by it (see, for instance, MacLachlan and Swartz 2009). Isn't it obvious that that is what aid and development are about? While many may accept that these are desirable downstream goals, however, people have quite honest intellectual differences about how to achieve them. Put simply, some accept that 'development' is uneven, and that it will first privilege those who are already relatively better off, and so have the resources to invest in projects that can ultimately produce better incomes for people further down the socio-economic ladder. In the category of those 'better off' may be the wealthy elites of low-, middle- or high-income countries, opportunistic multinationals or foreign governments with agendas that include the development of markets for goods produced in their own countries. So the idea here is that if the GDP tide can rise within a poor country, then eventually it will 'lift all boats', and because this has been achieved through market-driven change, it is often felt to be preferable, or 'better', or more sustainable than the alternatives.

Inclusive development is about trying to empower people who have been marginalized by, and/or are voiceless because of, a social/political/cultural system that promotes some interests over others. Of course, arguably, all systems do this. Women, persons with disabilities, ethnic minorities, sexual minorities, rural people and the poor are often outside the 'mainstream' flows of power, and therefore lack power in advancing their human rights. Barbery (2007: 76) suggests that 'Empowerment is the expansion of poor people's abilities to participate in, negotiate with, influence, control and hold accountable institutions that affect their lives.' This goes for all marginalized groups and should be one of the reasons for development (Sen 1999), not simply a down-the-line by-product of it. Here we are concerned with who is empowered and how this contributes to making aid result in real human development for the most disadvantaged.

Conclusion

In this chapter we have argued that for aid to be for people it has to be about people, and that means it has to consider what is important in their lives. In the next few chapters we will develop our argument that dominance, justice and identity are among the primary concerns which motivate humanity. Our brief consideration of aid history since the 1950s has suggested that the psychological triad of themes we have identified are ones that resonate with the troubled development of international aid relations, and that while elements of such relationships may have changed, at least some commentators find ample evidence of the persistence of some of their most pernicious undercurrents. It is to understanding these, and what can be done about them, that we now turn.

3 | Dominance

'Instituting a national aid programme has become a way for countries to proclaim their "developed" status. All OECD countries – and quite a few others – now have one ...' Moore (2007: 41)

'... any realistic vision of sustainable development must tackle the question of personal power relations head-on' Edwards and Sen (2000: 606)

In his book *The White Man's Burden* (2006), economist William Easterly argues that much, if not most, international aid is inept, economically. We argue that aid, and related development initiatives, are often inept, behaviourally. To be precise, they are often wrongheaded about human relationships. Much aid and development work, we suggest, is psychologically naive. Far from it being 'all hearts and flowers', an insufficiency of focus on human relationships has concrete consequences for aid in particular, and development in general.

Our starting point for this thesis is the idea of dominance. 'Dominance' means that the interests of one prevail over those of another. The intellectual apparatus we use to analyse dominance relations is Social Dominance Theory (Sidanius and Pratto 1999). According to the theory, human societies have an inherent motivation, rooted in prehistory and sociobiological evolution, to create and maintain structures that protect their own interests. Seizing and keeping the high ground are means to that end.

Homo dominicus is a different animal from *Homo economicus*. First, he is not just after wealth for its own sake; he wants the status that goes with it. Second, the goals are not just material but social as well. The high ground in question can be moral just as much as financial; by implication, those who serve the poor, at least in some cases, will quite literally want to lord it over them, too. Third, social dominance extends beyond purely individual motives (what some in economics call 'methodological individualism', or 'personal agency theory'). It also includes, of course, groups and institutions.

As is often said, 'there is nothing as practical as good theory', because if you can understand why something is the case, then you can use that understanding in other cases too. But, a warning – we need to disentangle our ego from our theory! When we are wrong we learn a lot. When we can't accept the possibility of being wrong, we are dangerous zealots, not contributors to development. We need to be wary of applying understandings from one context and culture to the problems of another context and culture (MacLachlan 2006). For instance, we have argued that in the case of many low-income countries, theories from elsewhere may be reconstituted (broken apart and put back together again with different understandings), restated (where a general theory may hold but it needs to be qualified, at least to some extent) and/or refuted (the theory is plain wrong, at least in this context). Finally it can be realized that a new theory has to be developed to explain what is going on (MacLachlan and Carr 1994).

Dominance in 'knowing what is best for' development

Curiously, those who write on and research the aid and development process rarely turn the spotlight on themselves and their own activities regarding how they contribute to aid and development. As researchers, that's something we wish to address in this book, because, as we know, 'knowledge is power'. Walpole (2007: 118) puts it more thoughtfully: 'Research is power and research shapes the world. Research is carried out to discover new facts and it is based on these facts that actions are taken. Research creates knowledge and hence creates power.' So let's briefly look at some very contemporary ideas about aid and development, and ascertain the extent to which elements of dominance might be at work there.

Abhijit Banerjee, a professor of economics at MIT's Abdul Latif Jameel Poverty Action Lab, recently laid out his stall in terms of what was needed to make aid work, and courageously invited commentary on his opinions from others. Banerjee's basic ideas were that much of aid thinking is 'lazy thinking', because people don't think through what is happening and, crucially for him, don't undertake randomized controlled trials of aid interventions; hence they don't really know what works. He also argues that the 'current fashion of channelling aid into broad budgetary support (rather than specific projects) in the name of national autonomy seems particularly disastrous' (Banerjee 2007: 21). Banerjee argues that the international community should return to financing specific projects, rather than giving money to central government for it to prioritize its use. The implication is that it's the donors who know best, not the recipient governments.

While all, we would hope, will agree with Banerjee on the importance of measuring the effects of interventions, and of using strong research designs (random control trials and others) to facilitate this, it is his judgment on those countries that question his view – his ideology – which is most disturbing: 'The guiltier the country [he doesn't say of what], the more it will protest that it needs the independence to make its own choices and that moving away from broad budgetary support undermines its suzerainty. But we owe it to their unfortunate and oppressed citizens to hold the line' (ibid.: 26).

The paternalism is clear: once again, the theme of saving the hapless citizens from their (usually) democratically elected governments, and applying the methods 'we know work best', is promoted; almost in the same breath as the enthusiastic recognition that '… the time is ripe to launch an effort to change the way aid is *given*' (ibid.: 24, emphasis added).

In our view, these ideas may be underpinned by the presumption of intellectual dominance – that the materially wealthier economies know best what to do and how to do it, that poorer governments should not be given funding directly into their exchequer so that they can decide on its best use, and that there is 'one best way' of evaluating what works best, and, yes, it's our way! We have probably overstated the point here and used Banerjee as an example of something that probably most higher-income-country academics are guilty of, at least some of the time. The point, however, is that researchers themselves are not above social dominance. The theory is self-reflexive.

What other kinds of hierarchy, exactly, is dominance theory talking about? According to the theory, hierarchies are chiefly based on age, on gender and on what are called 'arbitrary sets' (age and gender, according to the theory, are 'non-arbitrary', i.e. naturally given). 'Sets' in the definition above include groups, institutions and the inter-individual relations within them. 'Arbitrary' means socially constructed on anything other than chronology (age) or biology (sexed identity). Arbitrary sets therefore include, for example, race, class and caste. Arbitrary sets also incorporate power relations.

Power in general has a number of roots (Thibaut and Kelley 1959). These roots apply to aid and development (LeMieux and Pratto 2003). First, there is need among the poor to enter relationships but freedom among donors not to. Second, donors have freedom to set the price for exchange (e.g. the terms of an award, contract, services, etc.). Third, they have freedom to exit the relationship; hence aid work is paradoxical. By virtue of its own financing mechanisms and structures, aid often positions individuals, groups and institutions in hierarchies – even though, many would feel, it is supposed to break down the very asymmetrical privileges that such positioning implies.

To see why, let us put an earlier example under the dominance lens. Seen through this lens, the research network story in Chapter 2 becomes a reflection of power and privilege. Dominance permeates relationships within and between groups ('developed', 'developing', 'really underdeveloped' guys). It permeates relationships between 'developed' and 'developing' individuals (the attendees), and it permeates institutions (the league of universities and wider institutions, such as the research network and its sponsors). Put another way, social dominance theory is again critically self-reflexive.

It's the contradiction, stupid

Some years ago in Malawi, we encountered what anthropologists call a 'rich moment'. These are formative experiences, defining moments. In our case, a respected professor of education told us off – severely – for failing to see what was under our noses. Aid-funded workers receive heaps more money, in local terms, than their expatriate counterparts. Heaps meant roughly ten to twenty times the local salary. We discuss that issue in more detail in the next chapter. The point for now is that we had been missing the disparity. We had overlooked a very big issue, which was right under our noses. Let's be clear, we are not talking about CEOs or rock-star celebrities and what they earn. We are talking about people working right next to each other: peers and colleagues, theoretical equals, often with similar qualifications and experience. How could we miss such a glaring vertical gap, especially since so much of our research was supposed to be focused on levelling the field, on building, not undermining, capacity, etc.?

Intriguingly, the dominance perspective begins to suggest an answer; although it is one that many people, like ourselves above, initially won't want to hear. The answer starts from an idea that aid is partly working against the grain in human motivation, not simply with it. According to social dominance theory, the more aid strives to reduce human poverty, the more it may actually meet an equal and opposite, essentially social, reaction: maintaining, and even perhaps enhancing, the very gaps it finds so distasteful. Put slightly differently, aid is made up of, and is full of, internal contradiction.

Sometimes this may be so stark and so uncomfortable that aid workers may act as though they are 'splitting' their consciousness; being forced to coexist in an aid system that at once places them in situations of great need, suffering and perhaps even starvation, and at the same time in situations of great affluence, hedonism and overindulgence (MacLachlan 1993a). For example, on a recent trip to Addis Ababa, one of us was struck by the stark contrast in the juxtapositioning of a plush international hotel and a poverty-stricken man herding his goats literally ten yards from the door of the hotel. One is compelled to either treat these as two different worlds and accept them as such, or question whether one's own presence is contributing to, rather than reducing, this disparity. It may be a necessary defence to 'split the difference' in order to function effectively, and yet failure to question one's role and identity in the perpetuation of such disparity smacks of delusion.

According to social dominance theory, helping to shield people, often in quite subtle ways, from home truths, are myths. Our respected professor was telling us, in effect, 'Wake up to your*selves*, not just the system! Be mindful of the irony (and hypocrisy) in your immediate environment.' By challenging our complicity and naivety, the professor was challenging taboo. He was challenging what dominance theorists call '*legitimating* myths' (emphasis added). These are essentially rather self-serving fables, self-interestedly perpetuated by powerful and privileged groups, institutions and individuals. Myths help the powerful to justify the dominance that prevails, to collective, institutional and individual selves as much as to others. Mythology is therefore an everyday exercise in the power of self-delusion, and of self-deception.

In the case of aid expatriates (to give one example), the privileged may implicitly regard themselves as 'hero-innovators'. Hero-innovator is a narrative, an implicit storyline that one is living a great adventure. It is an example of what dominance theory calls 'paternalistic' myths (we serve society, look after incapable minorities, are changing the world). In 'reciprocal' myths, by comparison, everyone has equal opportunity. 'Meritocracy' myths, in turn, reassure us that anyone can make it if only they try hard enough. Pay gaps thereby become opportunities for the lower paid to earn more (a good thing), rather than ways to hold the privileged in place and the poorer down (a bad thing). In 'sacred' myths, some institutions, groups and individuals have a legitimate right to run the show.

More parallels in development work generally are easy enough to propose. Groups, institutions and individuals 'develop capacity'. They promote 'the free market'. They award 'prizes' for merit. They host 'development summits' that affirm rather than challenge a clear (if unspoken) 'expert-ocracy' (Dallmayer 2002).

All in all, dominance theory itself is quite challenging, quite 'contrarian'. It implies that aid systems are unwittingly glossing over reality. Hierarchy prevails, and is even reinforced by the activities of the system itself. In aid and development work, the theory predicts, two generally contradictory storylines will have to run at the same time: (1) all is well with the current hierarchy, because (2) it is not a hierarchy at all. Myths about meritocracy, free markets and the like help the privileged to believe that the world is a just place (Chapter 4). They reassure the folks in them – the worried well – that their position in the structure, vis-à-vis lower rungs, is OK. Challenging that kind of myth is taboo: it threatens the bubble; it touches a nerve.

What about the 'underdeveloped' guys?

The analysis just offered is mostly about the 'developed' guys. What about the 'underdeveloped' guys? Social dominance theory makes another, perhaps rather surprising, claim. The flipside of dominance is acceptance, or rather deference. Some of those 'under-developed' groups, institutions and, less so perhaps, individuals may actually 'internalize' an inferior position on the development ladder. At a meeting in Washington recently, a discussion on whether technical assistance should be continued prompted an African colleague to describe technical assistance as analogous to a parent nurturing a child (the implication being that the child is the recipient of the assistance). We do not plan to recount the history of technical assistance and its failings, but can't help but wonder why expertise travelling from high-income to low-income countries is termed 'technical assistance', yet the term is never used to describe the flow from low-income to high-income countries (professional experienced health workers from many African countries are, after all, providing technical assistance in many health systems in high-income countries). Frankly, social deference is not a new idea in development studies or other subject areas (e.g. Fanon's 1952 *Black Skin, White Masks*; Haley and Malcolm X 2001). As these and other social consciousness writers reveal, the disempowered often internalize some of their status as 'developing' rather than 'developed'.

There is a limit to that process, of course. First, there is a certain amount of sheer pragmatism to playing along with development assistance, in not biting the hand that feeds us. Second, groups nearer the bottom of a food chain may not be as satisfied with their lot as those feeding nearer the top (Sidanius et al. 2004). One of the things setting dominance theory apart, however, is an emphasis on both sides of the deference–dominance coin. The 'developed' are often at least mildly delusional; they have completed their 'development', compared to the 'developing world' (as if!). In fact, even within the 'developing' sets, there will be deference and dominance. Hierarchies are continua, they have multiple rungs. So the developing guys are likely to position themselves above some-one else. In this case, that someone else is likely to be the most marginalized of all. We will explore dominance theory further, but before doing so we consider a few examples of how dominance is practised in development.

No, I'm not going to show you the money!

We began this chapter by noting that the economist Banerjee had addressed the important issue of to whom donors should give their money – the governments of poor countries, or just to some groups within those countries? In fact development agencies are increasing the share of aid that is given as direct budget support. As the name suggests, direct budget support is financial aid that is given as a direct contribution to a partner government's budget. This may include a general contribution to the government's overall budget (general budget support), as well as contributions to the government's budget in specific sectors (sector budget support). A budget support approach to giving financial aid can be contrasted with project aid. Project aid is usually more specific and local-ized, with a focus on particular projects. So, (i) direct budget support and (ii) project aid are not just different types of financial transac-tion, they also embody different types of relationships between donors and recipients. Put simply, direct budget support allows the governments of poor countries to decide how best to use the money, whereas project aid allows non-governmental (or sometimes regional governmental) agencies to make such decisions. In the latter case the donor can therefore put certain conditions, or 'conditionalities', on its use, although this may also be the case with direct budget support. In Chapter 5 we return to this issue.

Econometrically, it has been argued that budget support is better than project aid when the preferences of donors and recipients are aligned (when they want to achieve the same things) and when the money transfers are relatively small in comparison to the recipients' own resources (Cordella and Dell'Ariccia 2007). Of course, these conditions often don't hold. Table 3.1 highlights some of the costs and benefits of direct budget support versus project aid.

TABLE 3.1 Planning balance sheet for project aid and direct budget support

Group	Project aid Cost	Project aid Benefit	Direct budget support Cost	Direct budget support Benefit
Donor government	High transaction costs Political cost of project failure	Generates local employment and income for local business community and consultants	Political risk Less control of budget allocations by recipient governments	Reduced transaction costs Improved efficiency and effectiveness of aid
Recipient government	Less autonomy and budget expenditure discretion Donor harmonization problem Parallel off-budget project management of aid project	Efficient project management by expats during construction/implementation phase Technology transfer through foreign projects Institutional strengthening through projects		Improved efficiency, effectiveness and public financial management Greater policy alignment of aid and predictability of aid flows
Recipient country Local citizens Customer	Unsuitable project design that fails to meet needs			Accelerated economic development Poverty reduction Better service delivery
Local suppliers	Reduced business			Increased business
Foreign suppliers		Increased income and employment	Reduced business	
Local consultants	Reduced business			Increased employment opportunities
Foreign consultants		Increased income and employment	Reduced employment and income	

Source: Reproduced by kind permission of McMaster (2008)

As McMaster states, 'the move from a Project Aid approach to Direct Budget support changes the power relationship between donor and recipient governments' (2008: 55). Our concern here is likewise less with the econometric algebra of success described in Cordella and Dell'Ariccia (2007), and more with the human dynamics of the power relationships that each approach implies.

Stepping back from the situation, do you recall your parents ever giving you pocket money, but restricting what you could spend on it? 'Yes, it's your pocket money, but you can't buy sweets with it!' The lack of discretion over the money and the lack of trust – you hadn't actually wanted to buy sweets with it – can undermine your relationship and your self-confidence. When a donor provides direct budget support to a local government they are saying 'we trust you to prioritize your spending in line with what needs to be done and we trust your estimation of what needs to be done'. Ownership of the 'gift' resides in the recipient government, and the donor might also invest in strengthening 'good governance' in the recipient country. When a donor seeks to fund specific projects, however, rather than routing their funding through the government treasury, they are saying, in effect, 'we don't trust your judgement of what needs to be done and/or we don't believe that you will do it anyway'.

This is symbolically undermining the central government, but there are ways they can get their own back. Aid is sometimes described as 'fungible', meaning that funding given for one purpose can be used for another. Let's say a recipient government plans to develop public health services in a particular region and a donor then gives funding to an NGO to provide such services in that region. Rather than the national government seeing the donor's project funding as additional funding to support public health services in the region, they may decide that the aid funding can be used instead of government funding, and divert their own funding towards other priorities. In this way, the donor's funding is effectively brought into the government's coffers by an alternative route. Project aid becomes budget aid, and the attempt at social dominance backfires (at least from the perspective of donors).

Aside from the huge scope for financial games, sometimes a much more fundamental social dominance 'game' is going on: 'who runs this country?'. Symbolically undermining the authority and ownership of a government – especially a democratically elected one – is likely to provoke a response that asserts the value and identity of the government (see Chapter 5). What much economic analysis misses is that it is the symbolism – what the flow of money represents – which is often more critical than the amount, or sometimes even what it is directed towards. If we want to address the negative effects of dominance in aid, we should be putting more funding through direct budget support, trusting our 'development partners' more, facilitating their 'ownership', but also providing support to promote good governance of such monies. The problem is that this approach can be slow and, more fundamentally perhaps, runs against the grain of a more general dominance motive.

Less against the grain, however, it is not difficult for aid agencies to identify a social problem and set up a focused project that can produce dramatic results within a few years in a contained area. Many NGOs secure funding to identify and address problems in this way. Thus, within specific projects antiretroviral medication can be made available to people with HIV/AIDS; school enrolment improved; water quality enhanced, and so on. At the end of the funded project, the gains are often not sustained, however, because they have happened in isolation from the mainstream health, education or sanitation systems. Aid projects that seek to strengthen central government systems that help prioritize action are certainly not as 'sexy', nor do they have such rapid effects, as short-term NGO-delivered projects. They may nonetheless offer a surer, but slower, path to improvement, where such improvements can be incorporated into and supported by systems that have been designed to do just that (MacLachlan 1996).

Of course, the human dynamics of these two alternatives (i.e. central versus local) could be somewhat straddled by a slightly different aid architecture. Multilateral donors could provide funding through direct budget support and recipient governments could contract local and international NGOs to undertake specific project work, also ensuring that it contributed to overall system strengthening. This would make NGOs more accountable to recipient governments, and give those governments greater ownership and control, but it would still also allow them to avail themselves of the undoubted benefits of the specific and needed skill sets that many NGOs can provide. Most importantly it would shift the sense of control over funding away from a dominant external donor to the recipient government. Although the latter would, of course, still have to account for the effective use of such funding. Dominance is not necessarily confined to international aid agencies.

Dominance behind insinuations of 'corruption'

What has influenced aid decisions for some time now is that recipient governments are often seen as at best inept, at worst corrupt, sometimes both. The aid-speak for such shortfalls is that host governments lack 'good governance'. So too, social dominance and recent banking sector debacles suggest, do many of the donors. A strong argument against direct budget support is that individuals in corrupt governments can use such 'unallocated' funds to their own self-serving ends. But the problem of corruption is much broader than which system of aid contribution is used. Corruption may be defined as 'the misuse of entrusted power for private gain' (Ewins et al. 2006: 7). Corruption, surely, is something we can all be against – like murder, global warming or the end of holidays. Corruption is also something that rich governments point to in poor governments, but rarely want to acknowledge in their own. A Zambian economist was visibly shocked when, on praising the 'miracle of the Celtic Tiger' – the rapid growth in the Irish economy from the mid-1990s to the mid-2000s – he was told of the level of corruption in the top level of the Irish government. During that period, Ireland had a minister for justice in jail, a former Taoiseach (prime minister) shown to be in receipt of substantial gifts (one, from just one individual, exceeding £1 million) and the then current Taoiseach (and former minister of finance) under investigation for corrupt practices, as a result of which he was subsequently forced to resign. Such practices the Irish government would not tolerate in the governance of countries that were the recipients of its aid programme. And, of course, it would be right not to tolerate them.

Finding out-and-out corruption is one thing, but perhaps the thin end of the wedge is accepting a lack of accountability and, perhaps not unrelated to this, the accountability of some of our most vaunted aid organizations. For instance, Vasquez argues that 'the World Bank and other aid agencies do surprisingly little to properly evaluate the impact of their projects' (2007: 47). Thus (even?) the World Bank may not always behave in the transparent and accountable manner which it demands from its clients.

Transparency International has highlighted the importance of addressing corruption in its 2006 report *Mapping the Risks of Corruption in Humanitarian Action*. They note that the context of humanitarian action and the nature of the action itself have a strong influence on the likelihood of corrupt practices. Corrupt practices will be influenced by, for instance, whether an emergency arises from a conflict or a natural disaster; is of quick or slow onset; how much international attention it receives; and the extent to which activity focuses on relief or reconstruction. Each of these contexts gives more or less scope for corrupt practices. Also, one's position in the aid hierarchy, or one's position of dominance, influences the opportunities for corrupt gains from the aid process. For instance, if a needs assessment is to be undertaken, this may present an opportunity for aid elites to influence assessors – assessors gain bribes and elites gain 'political capital'; that is, they cultivate a favourable impression in those they help.

At the level of consultation with local authorities, coercion may be used to influence the shape, size or location of a project, again allowing for the accumulation of political capital by certain authorities. In this process, needs may be inflated or certain social groups favoured, again allowing those in powerful positions to strengthen their influence. Moving a bit farther down the dominance hierarchy, decisions about the procurement of goods or services provide scope for inclusion/exclusion on a list of tenders and the awarding of contracts, contingent on bribes. At the level of distribution, there are, of course, risks that those involved will divert some of it for personal gain, including financial, sexual or material gain. When it comes to project monitoring, reporting or evaluation, false or exaggerated reports may be produced to secure continued funding or employment, or assistance for favoured groups. It is, nonetheless, important for us to stress, as do Transparency

International, that the corruption described in humanitarian aid is probably no greater or less than in any other sector, or within the societies in which the aid is provided; or perhaps within the societies from which aid is given.

Some 'aid corruption' may arise simply because the aid process places some people in dominant positions over others and allows them the opportunity to fulfil their greed. Some may be because it gives people who have too little to meet their needs (and extended family needs) the opportunity of getting more. Some may be because people see it as a means of hitting back at an unjust system – of secretly getting even; what they gain is perhaps less important than the sense of retribution. As we will see, they may also be rebelling against their felt injustice of being in a dominance relationship.

The UN Convention against Corruption is an important step towards creating an international framework to address and prevent corruption, but so too is the reform of the international aid system; reform that may reduce some of the motivation and some of the opportunity for corruption. Not sufficiently discussed in aid is the question of the relationship between corruption and waste, and between profligacy and mismanagement. Ewins et al. (2006) suggest that locals may consider the tendency to pay expatriates much higher than local salaries as profligate. A Transparency International survey in Bangladesh reported 'foreign donor officials staying in 5-star hotels and charging it to a disaster relief account' as corruption. Willits-King and Harvey (2005: 16) also note that the perceived efficacy of aid workers may colour the propensity for corruption:

> If local people see foreign organizations paying inflated prices for accommodation, vehicles and staff, staying in up-market hotels, and being overcharged by traders, while at the same time not delivering effective assistance, then they might conclude that it is legitimate to exploit them. 'Profligacy' and ineffectiveness may contribute to corruption at the local level.

They argue that this may be particularly likely in high-profile emergencies, which are characterized by a rapid influx of aid agencies, coordination problems, overlap and duplication, and competition for staff, along with some people driving up commodity prices.

Even something as basic as aid workers' salaries, it seems, reflects social dominance.

As the example above indicates, pay is not just about the money, or the utility you can buy with it. Sure, money has a practical value, particularly in impoverished communities, but it also has symbolic meaning. As we showed in a study in Malawi, even in an imaginary scenario where people have enough to live comfortably without having to work, most would still want to work (Carr et al. 1995).

A recurrent theme throughout this book will be the symbolic meaning of human actions. The symbolism of business-class fares, residing in posh hotels or zooming around in air-conditioned swanky vehicles is meant to convey something – dominance, either through justified achievement or purely in terms of the position one person is in relative to another. There are, however, some even more disturbing aspects of how dominance permeates international aid efforts.

Dominance, governance and the tangle of accountability

Growing concerns among donors about corruption, coupled with international pressure to pool resources and utilize instruments such as Direct Budget Support (DBS), has led to a focus on good governance. The World Bank sees governance as 'the traditions and institutions by which authority in a country is exercised for the common good'. This includes the process by which those in authority are selected, monitored and replaced, the capacity of the government to effectively manage its resources and implement sound policies, and the respect of citizens and the state for the institutions that govern economic and social interactions among them. The Ugandan government's Poverty Eradication Action Plan of 2004/05 defines good governance as: 'the efficient, effective and accountable exercise of political, administrative and managerial authority to achieve society's objectives including the welfare of the whole population, sustainable development and personal freedom' (Ministry of Finance 2004: 115).

Comparing the anticipated outcomes in these two definitions, 'the common good' versus 'promoting human welfare and positive transformation of society', the latter is more explicit but both raise the questions: Who defines? Who measures? To whom is the government accountable? In democratic nations governments are accountable to their citizens or public, and good governance entails transparency and responsiveness in this relationship. Donors who make aid conditional on good governance are thwarting this accountability relationship by creating a situation where governments are accountable to citizens or accountable for the 'common good' but accountable through the donor. This interjection in the accountability chain places the donor government or agency in a dominant position and in doing so undermines the identity of the recipient government, thus weakening its capacity for accountability to its citizens.

Moore (2001) makes the point that political 'underdevelopment' is about the disconnect between states and citizens. Poor countries tend to be relatively independent of citizens because they have access to unearned income (from donors) and there is less bargaining for the distribution of resources. He also places some of the blame on the donor community, who often compete among themselves in poorer countries and effectively undermine local processes. Moore is also critical of the conventional donor response to political underdevelopment – transferring their own political models and aligning institutions more closely with those in the North. He suggests that more attention needs to be paid to ways in which donors currently help to sustain political underdevelopment in the South, by perpetuating situations where state elites in the South can remain too independent of their own citizens.

To sum up, there is a paradox, a contradiction. In essence good governance places citizens in a dominant position. Donor agencies in their attempts to engender good governance remove the citizenry from that dominant position. In doing so, they can, in fact, undermine the fundamental nature of good governance.

Celebrity as dominance

We live in an age when celebrity entertainers dictate much of what the world thinks, feels and does. Moyo (2009) is critical of the effects of aid and argues that the 'pop culture of aid' has spawned many misconceptions. She claims:

Aid has become part of the entertainment industry. Media figures, film stars, rock legends eagerly embrace aid, proselytize the need for it, upbraid us for not giving enough, scold governments for not doing enough – and governments respond in kind, fearful of losing popularity and desperate to win favour. (Ibid.: xviii–xviv)

An extraordinary thing has happened; some of our best singers and actors – the world's dominant entertainment elite – have been allowed to influence development policy.

Celebrities may be people who are 'famous for being famous' or 'genuine stars', as the Hollywood elite might prefer to distinguish themselves. One thing is for sure – they assume socially dominant roles, usually in adulation, for their 'performances', on or off stage. Movie and rock stars now get to tread the hallowed hallways of global political power in ways for which drama school or voice training surely never prepared them. Bono and Sharon Stone attend global economic summits; Bob Geldof and George Clooney feed into United Nations deliberations, while these events are of course off limits to most elected representatives and just about all mere citizens. Perhaps it is not too outrageous to suggest that the music you pay to listen to, and the movies you pay to see, might in fact have a greater influence on shaping policy on world poverty than will your cherished democratic vote to appoint public representatives. There has been a mutation of dominance – rich entertainment elites are preaching on the relief of the impoverished proletariat – the train has jumped tracks.

It is easy to be critical of celebrities; people who possibly find personal meaning or greater fame through association with a cause that may seem to be the dimensional opposite of the professional roles and the private (or public) lifestyles they adopt. Yet such cynicism (see Table 3.2) also needs to be tempered by the recognition that celebrities, no less than anyone else, can use what they have to contribute to alleviating some of the world's most pressing problems. If celebrity is what you have, then there may be nothing wrong with giving a bit of it to a good cause, and drawing people's attention to an issue from which they would otherwise all too easily avert their gaze. In fact, we suspect that many celebrities are painfully aware

> **Box 3.1 Some thoughts on celebrity and international aid**
>
> 'Like everything else in Hollywood, philanthropic causes
> are susceptible to the fickle nature of celebrities, who are
> desperate to associate themselves with whatever happens to
> be the hippest, hottest issues du jour.' www.bestweekever.
> tv/2006/06/15/pollis-humanitarian-aid-the-new-aids/
>
> 'Celebrities are up there with pillars of the community – they
> are voices of influence.' Bronk, executive director of the
> Celebrity Coalition, an organization pairing celebrities with
> causes, 2002
>
> 'Politics and rock and roll don't go together all that well
> most of the time.' Niall Stokes, editor of the Irish music
> magazine *Hot Press*
>
> 'Celebrity and politics have merged. Today, well-heeled rock
> or movie stars cannot ignore the lure of association with a
> good cause; politicians cannot resist the call of stars whose
> message reaches an audience beyond politics.' Alan Cowell,
> *New York Times*, 1 July 2005

of the juxtaposing of their contribution to 'third world' causes
and the celebration of their 'first world' successes. Setting yourself
up for such criticism, motivated by a fundamental conviction, is
therefore potentially a courageous thing to do. But how useful is
it? What effect does it actually have on the public? Is this a good
use of dominance in aid?

Agrawal and Kamakura (1995) suggested that celebrities sell products by enhancing message recall, increasing recognition of brand
names and facilitating a positive attitude towards the brand. They
also claimed that despite some celebrities getting multimillion-dollar
payments for endorsing certain products, on average the impact
of celebrity endorsements on stock returns is positive, 'suggesting
that celebrity endorsement contracts are generally viewed as a worth-
while investment in advertising' (p. 56). More recently, Jackson and
Darrow (2005), exploring the effects of political statements made

by celebrities, found that young people's level of agreement with certain political statements was increased by celebrity endorsement and specifically that 'celebrity endorsements make unpopular statements more palatable, while increasing the level of agreement with already popular opinions' (p. 80). Celebrity endorsement thus seems to be capable of selling ideas as well as products. As suggested in Domino (2003), by the time of Princess Diana's fatal car crash in 1997 she had supported close to one hundred hospitals, charities, civic groups and humanitarian organizations, helping them raise an estimated $450 million each year. Hence celebrity dominance can pay in more ways than one.

In a street study we asked 100 Dublin commuters about their awareness of celebrity involvement in international aid activity. They were asked to name up to three celebrities. Of the 100 respondents, 99 per cent named at least one celebrity. Most of the sample (82 per cent) could name two celebrities, and about 45 per cent could name three celebrities. The most frequently cited celebrities were Bono, Angelina Jolie and Bob Geldof; the three together accounted for 72 per cent of the celebrities named. Bono alone accounted for 32 per cent of responses, and Angelina Jolie and Bob Geldof each made up about 20 per cent. The respondents consistently associated a narrow range of celebrities with international aid work.

Respondents generally, however, had difficulty in identifying concrete causes that celebrities espoused; most responses were very vague and encompassed a range of related issues (see Samman et al. 2009). Respondents were asked to identify up to three causes per celebrity and the causes were coded based on the keywords that the respondents gave; for instance, 'reduce poverty in Africa' was coded for both 'poverty' and 'Africa'. About 45 per cent could list at least one cause per celebrity, while in 20 per cent of cases respondents could not identify any message associated with the celebrity they had named.

In further analysis we found that most respondents felt the involvement of celebrities to be valuable in raising the profile of charities, though only a quarter of respondents (27 per cent) claimed to be personally influenced by such activity. The respondents were in fact fairly cynical as to the motives of most celebrities, whose

TABLE 3.2 Causes associated with most popular celebrities (%)

Specific cause	Bob Geldof	Bono	Angelina Jolie
Third World debt	27.3	26.1	1.7
Poverty	12.7	15.2	18.3
Hunger	16.4	5.4	1.7
Children	1.8	2.2	28.3
World suffering	14.5	9.8	8.3
Increased aid	1.8	2.2	3.3
Africa	10.9	13	8.3
Peace	5.5	3.3	0
AIDS/health issues	3.6	5.4	5
Other	0	4.3	1.7
Refugees	0	0	3.3
Don't know/unclear	5.5	13	20
TOTAL	100	100	100

Source: Samman et al. (2009)

involvement they felt served their own aims, namely publicity, first and foremost. In fact most of our respondents were more likely to be influenced by their perceptions of the character of the celebrity, rather than their causes. They respected celebrities they felt were genuinely committed to the causes they espoused, but, paradoxically, they felt such commitment was best demonstrated by the celebrity keeping a low profile, and by not actively seeking publicity. These may be anathema to the concept of 'celebrity' itself.

There are limits to perceived self-interest and aggrandizement, and therefore to the effects of celebrity aid. To offer your celebrity to promote a cause, and then for that cause to be compromised by criticism of and cynicism regarding your own behaviour, is undeniably problematic. For instance, a celebrity announcing an intention to go to Rwanda, and then not following through on it, is potentially very damaging as it casts the frenzied eye of publicity on poverty reduction in a whimsical way, thus actually undermining the 'worth' and dignity of people in need. Celebrity support is a tool to be valued and nourished. But the social dominance of celebrities needs to be carefully managed. Perhaps we need those celebrities who are truly committed – and there are many – to come together and develop a Charter of Good Celebrity Endorsement, especially as relates to issues of poverty reduction, natural justice and equity, so that celebrities too can, as Gandhi stated, 'be the change they seek'.

Dominance in organizations

At the beginning of this chapter we saw that social dominance theory encompasses three central elements: organizations, institutions and individuals. Of these three, perhaps organizations have been overlooked the most (www.humworkpsy.org/). A few years ago, when working in a government educational organization in a 'developing' country, we were acutely short of staff, even though positions were advertised internationally. Applicants wrote to the university administration, which was supposed to send us copies. Months went by without a word in response to a specific advert. Eventually the departmental head, an expatriate, was visiting the HR office. He spied in the bin, and picked up, an application. The applicant's human capital – the 'fundamentals' – was very good. The candidate was also neither local, nor from a wealthy economy. The application came from another 'low-income' country, a 'developing' economy in West Africa.

How is this example relevant to aid and development, and so to social dominance? At a basic level, we, like other departments, were perhaps missing out on good applicants. This represented serious downtime for the organization. Expatriates from lower-income regions, provided they have good fundamentals (as many do), are a promising prospect for organizations generally (Dore 1994): local salaries are regionally competitive; regional applicants know the conditions on the ground (they can hit the ground running); and they reduce reliance on costly expatriate aid from the wealthier economies (they are cost effective and perhaps more sustainable).

Expatriates from richer counties stack up less well, at least in some regards. They are less available for locally remunerated positions (the pay is poor), and less desirable on aid contracts (which are paid well), because dependence on aid is the inverse of what development should be about.

Despite all this, then, dominance in organizations may well have been increasing reliance on aid, while decreasing 'development' itself. Certainly from our departmental, group perspective at the time, the employing organization seemed to be behaving against its own best interests.

From a vantage point in social dominance, however, the picture is less irrational, more intelligible. We can imagine a hierarchy of countries of origin, not dissimilar to that in our opening story about the conference: 'developed', 'underdeveloped' and perhaps even 'really underdeveloped'. Perhaps the home country is positioned as underdeveloped compared to its really underdeveloped neighbours. Expatriates from wealthier economies, aid or locally salaried, are preferred over their really underdeveloped counterparts. The administrative group may have had an unspoken policy of discarding the really underdeveloped guys. This was not because of any genuine inability to do the job (i.e. fundamentals); it was precisely *because* they were positioned as really underdeveloped.

Anecdotes are not always reliable and, of course, we are acutely aware that some governments may be reluctant to employ some foreigners for fear of them inciting political unrest. There are a lot of ifs and buts in the equation. One way to improve the speculative nature of the analysis is to take another context altogether. Then we can check whether the same ground rules seem to apply.

Dominance in institutions

The East African Community (EAC) is a development institution, a regional trade bloc originally set up in 1967. It collapsed in 1977, but was relaunched via a new secretariat in 1996. Like all trade blocs, the EAC has been set up to facilitate free trade, including both goods and labour (regional expatriates) between Uganda, Kenya and Tanzania. Creating an institution such as the EAC can, in principle, create a freer market, liberalize trade and organizational performance and, ultimately, reduce reliance on international aid.

Shortly after the 1996 relaunch of the EAC, an opportunity arose to conduct a more systematic study of what we think we saw in the original anecdote. The new study was hatched with colleagues at the University of Dar es Salaam, who co-designed a survey about the EAC for Tanzanians (Carr et al. 2001). According to dominance theory, we might expect to see a similar pattern. Well-qualified expatriates from outside the home country but inside the trade bloc will be rejected in favour of equally qualified candidates who just happen to come from richer, more 'developed' country sets.

We approached Tanzanians with work experience, studying for a degree in commerce. They were asked how Tanzanian selection panels, in their experience, might process job applications. A series of simulations were run. The fictitious applicants all had equally good fundamentals. They varied, though, in one regard: their country of origin. Some came from outside Tanzania but inside East Africa; others originated from outside Tanzania but from higher-income, Western economies. Included too were candidates from inside the home country, Tanzania. The jobs at stake covered a range of occupations, all strategic for national development. They ranged from community worker through to engineer, educator and medical professional. To assist the participants in being frank rather than souls of discretion, we asked them to report from experience of others' behaviour, not their own. Such techniques can help people to be a little more candid, and speak freely. To mimic actual selection procedures, we asked them to rank the candidates according to how each might fare, based on their own experience, and local insights.

What should we find? On the one hand, the candidates are presented as equally skilled, and equally costly to relocate, etc. So we should expect no difference in the average rank predicted for each country of origin, across all jobs as a whole. In an ideal world, preferences should flatline. There will be no clear preference for any one country of origin over the next: a level playing field. On the other hand, any significant departure from a flat line possibly indicates a group-level bias.

Figure 3.1 plots the average rank predicted across all jobs, against the country of origin (home country Tanzania, expatriates from East Africa, and expatriates from the West). The figure signals some differences between the countries of origin: expatriates from economically more dominant nations appear to have an unfair advantage over expatriates from 'across the border'. In fact, the expatriate from the EAC has a statistically lower chance of being selected, all else being equal, than his or her counterpart from Tanzania. No such bias exists against expatriates from 'the West'. Why is that?

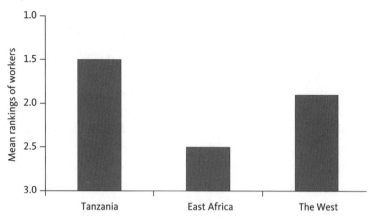

Note: 'The West' refers to recognized geographic countries of origin with relatively higher incomes. Expatriates from these sources were common at the time

FIGURE 3.1 An inverse resonance effect in Tanzania
Source: adapted from Carr and Coates (2003)

The findings are at least broadly consistent with social dominance theory, and with our earlier anecdote from Malawi: despite being well qualified to do the job, the 'really underdeveloped guy' is not getting a fair go, compared to the local candidate – a comparative disadvantage not experienced in Figure 3.1 by candidates from higher-income, OECD countries.

We do not wish to cast any aspersions on the EAC. Critics of the study, for instance, could point out that the participants were not representative of any general public or citizenry (they were all students). Nor did it measure social dominance of the countries directly and, of course, there may have been many other contextual factors at work. Related research in a different context, therefore, could be very informative.

Recognizing broader issues of institutional dominance at the highest levels is not difficult, or even contentious these days. The G8 is one example which can, of course, expand to include a greater number of dominant powers (G20), depending on the agenda of the controlling players. Likewise, the UN Security Council, with its five permanent members – the USA, Russia, China, Britain and France – and their veto-wielding powers, is hard to reconcile with a modern world where at least two of them (France and Britain) are now much more modest players on the world stage than was the case in the immediate aftermath of the Second World War. Even these five, however, can be bypassed if the relevant power is dominant enough – as was evidenced by a 'coalition of the willing' waging an unsanctioned war on Iraq. Onunaiju (2009), writing in the Nigerian paper *Daily Trust*, takes a somewhat sober but charitable view of the chronically troubled and troublesome UN systems in seeing it as a work in progress and not an end-state of global governance, but he notes: 'the United Nations has been quite relevant at least on the soft issues, such as education, health, human rights, etc. … but has buckled on the hard issues of equitable global economic order, militarization and war and has tragically looked on helplessly, as its most powerful members trample on those ideals on which it pronounced its moral and political anchor' (p. 21). While the election of Nigeria for a two-year period as a temporary member of the Security Council is noteworthy, it is nonetheless tinkering around the edges of a system of global dominance that is meant to promote the few, often at the expense of many.

Dominance against individuals

The examples above concern human mobility. For many years, scholars and policy-makers have debated the 'brain drain' of skilled migrants from 'developing' to 'developed' nations. The tack in the debate has visibly shifted, not only to South–South mobility, but also to the potential benefits of South–North movement, for the sending countries. The rhetoric has become noticeably more positive. Funders, for example, seem to want to hear about the potential benefits from migration to richer countries. Can benefits accrue not only to the richer countries, but also to the poorer, sending countries too? This is a rhetorical question. The rhetoric is win-win. A new ethos requires a fresh name. The new name is 'migration–development nexus'. Whether it comes via extended remittances, or through 'brain gain' to be had by return migration or 'the diaspora option', the implicit message is the same: migration can complement aid. It can fuel development, both in countries already developed (spot the contradiction) and also in those developing.

Clearly migration can benefit poorer communities in some ways. No one doubts this, and much scholarly effort has gone into pinpointing precisely how and where (e.g. Katseli et al. 2006). But social dominance theory suggests there might be another myth in the making here. One of the signs of such myth-making would be any nose-on-the-face oversight or blind spot.

One particular blind spot is glaringly obvious. For any migration to work, the migrant has to find work, and especially work that fits his or her actual brainpower (fundamentals). Indeed, many highly skilled and experienced migrants leave their developing home economy on the promise of a better life, primarily through a better job, in a new, wealthier economy. When they arrive, however, they either fail to find work that matches their qualifications, or they take many years to regain full employment, if ever, in the same career. Instead of brain gain or even brain drain (which at least implies a flow-on effect to somewhere), the outcome is lose-lose: a 'brain waste' (Mahroum 2000).

Brain waste takes two principal forms. When a doctor cleans toilets instead of landing a job in surgery, they are said to experience 'access bias' (access to proper employment). When they do succeed in finding a job but still encounter impediments (to promotion, bonuses, career development, etc.), they are said to experience 'treatment bias'.

What determines who proceeds and who gets blocked? One divider is where you have come from. Take a country like New Zealand, for example. Like other less populous OECD countries, New Zealand is heavily dependent, economically and socially, on a regular influx of skilled migrants. The New Zealand economy currently loses almost as many skilled people to emigration as it gains, annually, from immigration. At the same time there remains, in certain contexts within New Zealand, a culture of prejudice and discrimination against skilled migrants from some regions. Those regions include Asia, Oceania and Africa. Biases like that are bound to hurt national development sooner or later, at source and destination country alike. Whether the pain is group-based (e.g. organizations and families), institutional (e.g. professions) or individual (the skilled immigrant him- or herself), 'brain waste' is not good.

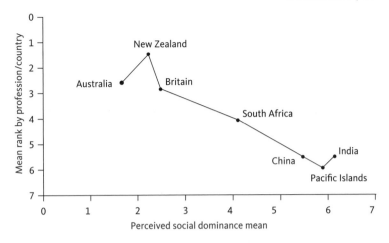

FIGURE 3.2 Perceived social dominance in different countries
Source: Coates and Carr (2005)

What is not in dispute, anywhere in New Zealand, is that skilled migrants from some sending countries, compared to other countries like Britain and the United States, meet bias. There are ample reports of its existence in New Zealand, including government statistics, etc. Less well understood, however, and largely overlooked, is why such biases occur in the first place.

Could social dominance be part of the picture? Figure 3.2 offers a first glimpse of what might be in play. It summarizes the combined wisdom of a range of subject-matter experts who provided the data. These people had on average more than ten years of witnessing and observing selection panels make decisions. Those decisions were often about evenly balanced candidates, from a range of different economies of origin.

Figure 3.2 summarizes what these experts in selection told us would probably happen if these candidates were head to head and had equally good 'fundamentals'. At the time in New Zealand, there was a skills shortage in the local labour market, so there was little or no purely logical reason for the jobs market to be behaving irrationally. Rationally speaking, in fact, the link between (i) country of origin on the one hand and (ii) employment prospects on the other should be non-existent; the line should be completely flat and even.

The stand-out feature in Figure 3.2 is that the slope is not at all level. There is a highly visible (and statistically significant) tendency for candidates from Australia, New Zealand and Britain to be favoured over those from South Africa, which is in turn preferred over China, the Pacific Islands and India. Skilled immigrants from wealthier sending countries are predicted by the experts to prevail.

Crucially, the same subject-matter experts were also asked to give their opinion about the level of social dominance for each sending country. Based on advice from the authors of social dominance theory itself about how to measure country hierarchies in people's minds, they were asked for a judgement based on best living standards, education, health and levels of wealth. From Figure 3.2, the data are consistent with social dominance theory. Chances for the migrant to secure the job reduce with several successive decrements in ranked social dominance. There is thus a fairly clear (and to reiterate, statistically significant) link between how dominant the sending country is perceived to be, and how well the immigrant from that country is likely to do at job interview.

The line in Figure 3.2 is not perfectly straight. Dominance (of course) is not the only way in which the countries of origin vary. For example, the sending countries are different from each other, and from New Zealand, in terms of culture, too. Could access bias be attributable, at least in part, to cultural similarity? Of course it could. Preferences we found also co-varied with the perceived degree of cultural similarity between the sending country and the host. British immigrants (for instance) had improved access compared to Asian ones, again roughly in proportion to the degree of similarity perceived to exist between the pairs of cultures concerned.

As we might expect, then, both dominance and similarity complement each other; they co-contribute to the effects observed. This confluence was captured well in the reasons that respondents gave for the access biases they predicted. One theme emerging from content analysis was prejudice against countries of origin (18 per cent), whose standards of living are perceived by job selectors in organizations as 'inferior' (15 per cent). Exemplary comments include 'typically waspish background and values', and 'There is a high level of ignorance regarding education and qualifications in places like India and

China'. These suggest social dominance – candidates, who objectively match others in their degree of fit to the job, are discriminated against via downgrades of their qualifications. Also emerging from the analysis was dissimilarity–similarity (27 per cent of responses). Exemplary comments include 'likes attract', and 'recruit in own image'. Both themes, similarity and social dominance, are encapsulated in the remark: 'They [HR and line managers] feel that people who come from a *standard of living* most *similar* to New Zealand will fit into the environment more easily' (Coates and Carr 2005: 590, emphases added). Culture, then, is not the only story.

The findings in Figure 3.2 relate to access, not treatment, bias. Social dominance theory, though, has been tested with respect to both forms. A good example can be found in work by Lim and Ward (2003). Their research also focused on a wholly different region. Their research study examined job and career prospects among skilled migrants moving from China and the USA to Singapore (ibid.). Just as in the study from New Zealand, despite demand for skills, there was bias. The candidates from China, with equally good fundamentals, were not only less preferred but also less well treated than applicants from America: the twin bias held for both access and treatment bias, in the latter case over retrenchment.

Overall, therefore, dominance can be linked to individual perception. Selection consultants see it second-hand; skilled immigrants experience it more directly. If skilled migrants are experiencing access and treatment bias as a result of social dominance, then the rhetoric of a migration–development nexus, one that complements development aid, is mythical. Social dominance relations, between rich and poor, have a potential to undermine any migration–development nexus. This is not to deny that migrants can earn more abroad, but rather to attest to the likelihood that they are still subject to the implicit dominance relationships imposed on them by others, and other socio-political systems.

Exposing a bias has the potential to help reduce it. In the Netherlands, for instance, awareness-raising training has reportedly been used to help address employer bias, and brain waste in particular (Evers and Van der Flier 1998).

The system

If some East African organizations screen out other African expatriates, that might enhance the organization's own dependence on aid (expatriate aid, or 'technical cooperation'). Institutions in higher education, like regional trade, function suboptimally. Freedom of labour is curtailed. Individual applicants from Africa can become disaffected and head elsewhere, contributing to brain drain and brain waste. These have a potential to trickle back 'up' the system, accelerating recruitment shortages in organizations and ultimately institutions, across developing and developed nations alike. Thus social dominance is multilevel, spanning groups, institutions and individuals. Those elements in turn form an interactive system. How might such a system work beyond the access and treatment biases already considered? In addition to asking for individual rankings of social dominance, Coates and Carr also consulted the Human Development Indicators compiled by the United Nations (United Nations 2003). These indicators entail life expectancy at birth, adult literacy rate, rates of educational enrolment, GDP per capita, etc. The various numbers are combined into an overall 'Human Development Index', or 'HDI'.

Curiously enough, in the New Zealand study, ranks listed in this HDI matched almost perfectly the rank order given by our subject-matter experts (in HR practices). Could such indices be fuelling social dominance? That would be ironic. According to social dominance theory, however, it is possible – and even likely – that institutional expressions of hierarchy (like the HDI) are not just neutral indicators of poverty and privilege. They are also potential drivers of the hierarchical relations between organizations and individuals, an arbitrary set in themselves. All research, including researched indicators like the HDI, has a social function, a consequential validity – even if that function is sometimes unintentional social dominance. Such being the case, the HDI and other indicators may, at least at times, be self-fulfilling prophecies.

Context

Dominance orientation is not always fixed but sensitive to social context. Put simply, it requires constant priming. Unfortunately the wrong (dominance) primes are everywhere in aid work. Everyday work conditions are loaded up with privileges (and deprivations) of one kind or another. Gaps in status, wealth, etc., are 'in your face'. Whether they like it or not, foreign aid workers move around in air-conditioned vehicles. They stay in good-quality accommodation, at least compared to their local counterparts. They draw higher salaries and benefits than their local counterparts. They have better access to medical care, education for their children and life prospects generally. They get to leave the poverty of their environment at the end of the assignment. They have decent career prospects, and a reasonable life expectancy. Many of these, admittedly unwanted, privileges are not shared by their colleagues from the host community.

Rankings like these are not the same as cross-cultural differences. They are less easily negotiated away. Humour doesn't really help. The reasons for the strata may well be perfectly rational and reasonable, to some expatriates at least. International aid groups also have legal and moral obligations to their employees, and international salaries have to be competitive in the wealthier markets. But there remains a heavy irony about the contradiction that aid working conditions often mirror the very gaps they are meant to dispel. According to social dominance theory, contradictions like these may reinforce and accentuate the hierarchy, not attenuate it.

Socialization

One of us recalls meeting a newly arrived aid expatriate, a radical socialist. He disparaged expatriate institutions as symbols of colonialism. One year later, however, the same expatriate had made a drastic turnaround. He was a stalwart chairman of the local gymkhana club – an expatriate-dominated social club that is a leftover from colonial times; he was even the chairman of it. More recently, in a discussion about salary discrepancies between expatriate and local staff, an experienced expatriate angrily suggested that a pecking order, with expatriates on far higher salaries, gives the locals 'something to aspire to'. Perhaps there is something vaguely off key, and telling, with outbursts like these (they are common enough). First, the probability that locals will reach expatriate heights (salary-wise, etc.) is unrealistic. We have learned that in our research with colleagues in Oceania. Second, even if they do, the system itself will not change: research with underprivileged groups and the individuals within them suggests that individuals who move up the hierarchy more often serve to sustain rather than challenge the hierarchy itself (Sidanius et al. 2004). Individuals, it seems, are likely to develop loyalties to the top rather than the bottom of a pyramid. At a recent humanitarian conference, we learned that some skilled local workers paid derisory local wages will eventually make it into the UN salary brackets – or what a consultant once described to us as 'the UN gravy train'. Gravy trains, however, can help to maintain social dominance, not combat it.

Protestations that all is well in the aid-world are, then, perhaps, reflections of mythology, of rationalized contradictions. A little bit of mythology helps the hierarchy go away. Myths offer the believer a way out. The truth, of course, has to be left unspoken, tacit, taboo. Otherwise, the illusion is gone, or at the least a nerve is exposed. To go back to our introduction to social dominance, vitriolic protestations that the natives have a fair go reflect at least two legitimating myths: equal opportunity and meritocracy. In reality, of course, what prevails, and what aid workers are socialized into, is an *expatocracy*.

Expatocracy

Socialization implies an ideology, and beyond that a culture, to be socialized *into*. Aid work has its culture like any other occupational domain. To lay out a culture of aid work, we need some help from workplace anthropologists. They have written about both organizational and occupational culture. A leading figure describes these as having three layers (E. Schein 1990). A first layer comprises the visible artefacts and rituals of the group, institution or individual. These may be the four-wheel-drives and health benefits. A second layer comprises the values and other goals that the groups, institutions and individuals aspire to in theory, in words. These are mission statements, Millennium Development Goals, calls to action and various summit declarations. That level is where the myths reside. A third and relatively deeper level comprises the implicit assumptions, i.e. underlying beliefs that may be just too difficult to voice, even to oneself. These harbour the taboo subjects, the contradictions, like the implicit suspicion, nagging doubt and sensitivity that a 'free' market is in fact neither free nor meritocratic. Deeper down, we know it is expatocratic, an expatocracy.

Exploring why some initiatives fail or do not achieve their intended outcomes, Coghlan and McAuliffe (2003) assert that the failed initiative 'is likely to have violated some taken-for-granted assumptions that are embedded in the organizational psyche because they were successful in the past' (p. 50). This, we believe, is the key. Many of those deeper-level assumptions are hidden, i.e. tacit. They have been passed on through generations, embedded in the psyche of 'aid culture'. They are most likely baggage from colonial times, when dominance was considered an essential ingredient to making things work. The air-conditioned four-wheel-drives and four- or five-star hotels are manifestations of implicit assumptions. The articulated values are camouflage for the same assumptions and artefacts. They paint the aidscape in softer, more palatable tones.

According to thinkers in organizational learning, however, aid work is doomed unless these tacit assumptions are unearthed, and the contradictions resolved. Their resolution is twofold. As with unbiasing job selection panels, a resolution requires first of all becoming aware of the tacit assumptions and the contradictions that exist between these and espoused values (Argyris 1999). Second, it requires *doing* something to break their self-perpetuating cycles (Senge 2002). The first task is probably easier to achieve than the second. From access bias to aid dependency, from migration to brain waste, and from aid to a culture of expatocracy, social dominance is at the core of that challenge. The applicability of social dominance theory is elementary. It helps uncover how and why groups, institutions and individuals don't really do what they say they should do. Exposing that contradiction enables us to begin to move forward.

A culture *myth*

Organizational and occupational culture is one thing. Societal culture is another. When international aid workers are preparing to go on international assignment, they may be lucky enough to receive pre-departure cross-cultural training. Such preparation is seldom afforded to the workers who will host the expatriates, and with whom the expatriates are intended to 'develop capacity'. When one of us worked in remote Far North Australia, training 'Balanda' (non-Aboriginal community workers) would irritate community leaders. They could not understand the one-sidedness of the equation. Why was there no 'pre-arrival' training and preparation?

Perhaps this one-sidedness reflects a hierarchy of its own. An even more intriguing question, however, is why sociocultural training is at least partially provided, whereas socio-economic training is not. It is as if many of the difficulties in aid work are attributed to culture, not privilege. We feel that this is a hiatus. It partly reflects the barriers for any aid system, posed by imbalances that typically prevail on the ground. Ultimately those hierarchies render aid work more difficult than it already is, not just for locals but for an expatocracy as well.

Viewed from a social dominance perspective, any emphasis on cultural training reflects mythology of its own. One myth we have already seen: cultures in lower-income countries are primitive, in need of development (Chapter 2). A second storyline is that cultural differences are what divide the camps, not material privation and privilege. Letting locals 'in' might threaten that bubble. The mythical element in the narrative is that there *is* no hierarchy, no ironic replication of poverty and wealth inside aid itself. Cultures, after all, are free to differ; that is their beauty. That beauty, that backwardness, has to be preserved. So culture training focuses on preparing the expatocracy to manage the natives, not the other way round.

The culture myth is that differences in aid and development work are cultural, not dominance based. Fix the cultural differences and we fix the relationship issues that dog some development projects and programmes. This ensures that the four-wheel-drives and the gravy train continue to roll. To paraphrase from Chapter 2, a culture myth implies that the culture of a country is its most important descriptor in matters socio-economic (a pseudo-indicator, we believe). This ignores the fact that an average culture profile hides huge individual and institutional differences. It implies that assistance should be targeted at modernizing cultures thousands of years old, rather than improving human rights, access to health services or educational provision.

An additional difficulty is that cultural training focuses on educating the expatriate about the host culture in the abstract, unwittingly encouraging the expatriate to become an observer of the host culture. This stance of observer creates a 'them' and 'us' divide that fails to recognize that the expatriate interacts with the host culture, and becomes part of the system he/she observes (Carr et al. 1998). This is a classic organizational problem that creates divisions between management and staff, and staff at different levels of the organization, and even system. The donors blame the NGOs; the NGOs blame communities – failing to recognize that they are all part of the same system. The system's ability to adapt and change can be significantly enhanced if members of the system at every level can connect their own actions with others' reactions (Coghlan and McAuliffe 2003).

Sure, to ignore the scale of the differences in cultural values would not be helpful. Cultural training should naturally continue, provided culture is understood as a dynamic environment into which the expatriate steps, not something static that can be observed and understood in the abstract. But let us stop hiding hierarchy behind culture. Let us stop blaming things on culture, a cultural attribution error.

Dominance is not everything

Hierarchy is equally, if not more, fundamental in poverty reduction than is culture. It interacts with cultural differences, and may even set them off. One feeds the other. Social dominance theorists themselves have been among the first to concede that dominance theory does not explain everything. In particular, it does not address the reality (thank goodness!) that societies, including power relationships, change. Revolutions happen, prejudice gets reduced, and hierarchies can be dismantled. Social dominance as an idea – a sharp edge in the aid triangle – helps expose the taboos, the hidden assumptions and inherent contradictions. To that extent, it may actually help to raise awareness of some of the key issues that hamper aid and development initiatives. But the theory comes up short as regards where to go from there. In the remainder of the book, we explore how two particular motives, justice and identity, can serve as levers for change.

We are also aware of a developing literature on the role of power in international aid, human rights and development (see, for instance, Hayden and Mmuya 2008). This is clearly related to the idea of dominance, as we have described it above. Power and dominance are not, however, synonymous; while some people clearly do have much greater power (of whatever type) than others, they can choose whether they will use that power to dominate others, or in fact to empower them to address inequity. Similarly, people can exercise influence without authority (Cohen and Bradford 2005) or influence without power (Ungerer 2007); perhaps softer versions of dominance without power. In this book our interest in dominance is relational (how people relate to one and other), rather than in resource-based power, although we fully recognize that the two are very often connected.

Conclusion

Nobody doubts or questions the motives and sincerity of many players in aid and development systems. Yet social dominance theory offers a potentially fresh, if somewhat challenging and controversial, perspective on aid and development work. The theory, and the research supporting it, suggests that the stratification of relations is a key impediment to development. Moreover, much of the stratification will be unwitting and unintended.

Intrinsic motivation, sincerity, dominance; there is evidently more than one human factor at play in development work. In particular, people, and the behavioural systems and institutions they house, contain contradictions. The desire for a level playing field and at the same time to win, to stay 'on top', are contradictory, even adversarial. Adversarial dynamics are one way to win the battle yet lose the war. Aid and development would be wiser if it heeded that advice, and recognized *Homo dominicus* for what s/he is.

4 | Justice

'Social injustice is killing people on a grand scale' Marmot (2008)

'Few things kill an individual's motivation faster than the feeling that someone else is getting a better deal. Organizational justice principles state that in addition to being fair, the people who make decisions must be *perceived* as fair. ... Thus this ... is arguably as much about leadership as it is about employee motivation' Latham (2007: 95, emphasis added)

'... at Oxfam we define poverty as social injustice rather than the absence of public goods or services. Our ultimate goal is to reduce the power imbalances that limit the poor from accessing such goods and services while empowering them to defend their economic and social rights' Offenheiser and Jacobs (2007: 101)

'If the misery of the poor be caused not by the laws of nature, but by our institutions, great is our sin' Charles Darwin

Wilkinson and Pickett (2009) have recently reviewed a large body of scientific health research, and their conclusions have clear political implications. Those countries which have more equal societies have healthier populations and fewer social problems and, in general, this is independent of absolute levels of income. How wealth is distributed between people matters. In fact, it is a life-and-death issue, not only in terms of resources available to address problems that arise, but also because inequitable social structures appear to actually create such problems. Our institutions, not nature, need to change. The Commission on the Social Determinants of Health was established by the World Health Organization in 2005, and submitted its final report in 2008. The Commission, constituted from leading health researchers, practitioners and policy-makers from around the world, made three broad recommendations: (1) improve the daily living conditions of the most impoverished; (2) measure and understand health problems and assess the impact of interventions; and (3) tackle the inequitable distribution of power, money and resources. This last recommendation applies to all aspects of human and social development, and is therefore much wider than health. It thus provides a core focus for this chapter.

The chapter is about a justice *motive*. Specifically, we argue that justice not only has to be done, it has to be seen to be done; our actions must be just and symbolize justice. Our comparison points are inside the aid system itself, compared to the wider population it serves. Yet inside aid work the justice motive is often overlooked. That oversight, we believe, compromises development projects, often from their outset. A greater understanding of justice perceptions and their impacts at group, institutional and individual level is critical if aid is to benefit the most disadvantaged.

More corruption

Picking up the theme of good governance again, a revealing, motivational analysis of governance issues at work can be found in a World Bank paper (Ferrinho and van Lerberghe 2002). These researchers focus on management in public health. They also suggest, however, that their analysis applies to sector-wide approaches in general (p. 19). The essence of their argument is that characterizing civil service organizations, institutions and individuals as 'corrupt' is naive. Close inspection, these authors reveal, starts to expose a plethora of human disincentives with which people are grappling.

Featuring prominently in the disincentives is a broken promise about the extent to which the state values its civil servants. There are big salary gaps with private sectors. There is a dearth of either performance or career incentives. And there is a sheer lack of resources to do the job. On top of all this, or rather underlying it, public sector salaries 'are most often "unfair"' (ibid.: 4). Under such conditions of unfairness, i.e. injustice like this, Ferrinho and van Lerberghe argue, 'demotivation, overall lack of commitment and low productivity are to be expected' (ibid.: 4).

The consequences of workplace injustice do not stop there. It has consequences for poverty reduction itself; it impacts on levels of human service to wider communities: 'To compensate for un-realistically low salaries, health workers rely on individual coping strategies' (ibid.: 5). Coping strategies like these are well known in organizations generally. In low-income government settings, according to Ferrinho and van Lerberghe, they can include absenteeism, under-the-counter payments and 'fee-splitting' (referring to a particular specialist clinician for a share of the fee). Coping strategies, like salaries themselves, are 'taboo' (p. 5). Nor are they confined to individuals; hospitals, for instance, may charge illegal fees as a way of meeting the costs of publicly needed supplies (p. 2).

As the example suggests, motives behind coping strategies are not necessarily bad or immoral. Often enough, in fact, they are more like rational responses to irrational demands. Salary, for instance, is not the only, nor the most important, motivator for many of these workers and groups. Many stay in office, serving the public, despite pressures to join a more lucrative private sector position. Social responsibility, professionalism, a sense of vocation and prestige play key retaining roles. In our recent study of health workers in Malawi (Manafa et al. 2009), the employees indicated that they were encouraged to take jobs as health professionals because of the opportunity to assist mankind, coupled with a spirit of patriotism. Most of the managers we interviewed believed that health workers were motivated to take up careers in the health sector as a personal choice, for the dignity that went with the profession, good career prospects, and on humanitarian grounds. Even reselling of drugs may have a partly social orientation – for example, sidestepping bureaucratic and costly delays (Ferrinho and van Lerberghe 2002: 4). Under such circumstances, labelling behaviour as mere 'moonlighting', or worse still 'corrupt', sells many workers short.

Ferrinho and van Lerberghe stop short of describing the behaviour of the protagonists as justice-restoring. They stick to 'justifying' rather than justice per se. Yet an even closer look, via justice theory, suggests a range of ways in which moonlighting *can* be seen, not only as a rational and reasonable response in general, but specifically as an attempt to restore justice. That said, 'justice' is a very broad concept, so let's now break it down into different types, with a particular emphasis on the work environment.

Types of justice

Since the 1960s, a great deal of systematic research has focused on deciding how many types of justice feature in everyday work behaviour in general. The settings span institutions and organizations like banks and schools, and the minds of those individuals who work in them (Colquitt et al. 2001). By and large, a reasonable consensus has emerged, at least within the work studies literature itself. What follows are the main types of justice that deserve consideration.

TABLE 4.1 A taxonomy of work justice

Distributive	Procedural	Interactional
Equity	Inclusive (voice)	Informational
Need	Probity	Interpersonal
Equality		

Distributive justice This simply means how the proverbial pie is sliced. Resources can be distributed in three different ways: equitably, where the ratio of outcomes to inputs is maintained – those who work harder get paid more; a meritocracy. Alternatively they can be based on need, including positive discrimination or affirmative action. Third, everyone gets the same, regardless of their contribution or inputs. This equality means that for disadvantaged groups or individuals, they get more than in an equitable system. Here we are not just talking about pay or rewards, but also the distribution of workload and responsibilities.

We might expect individuals to differ in the extent to which they endorse one of these systems over another. Within a given economy or economic subsystem, however, it is likely that a reasonable majority will gravitate towards one of these systems.

Of course, things get much more complicated when individuals, or groups (such as aid agencies), work across cultures, where there may be significant differences in what most people see as the 'fairest', or 'best', system to distribute resources, rewards or salaries. Cross-cultural researchers have found that distributive preferences are socialized somewhat differently in different settings (Carr 2003). For example, need may be more heavily socialized in poorer, or more collectivistic, societies; equity in wealthier, and in more individualistic, economies. Preferences may also shift depending on context – for example, from equality (everyone gets the same) and need when dealing with in-groups (your 'own people'), to strict equity (reward for effort) when dealing with out-groups ('them'), also known as 'othering'. Somewhat counter-intuitively perhaps, any tendency to deal with out-groups according to a strict equity rule may be more prevalent in collectivist than in individualist-oriented societies.

In the light of this analysis, so-called 'moonlighting' behaviour is clarified. Lower-than-expected remuneration can be seen as triply unjust; it is inequitable, it overlooks need, and it is inegalitarian (between public and private sectors). Aid agencies may compound this injustice by operating according to a need-based value system in how they target aid, but insisting on an equity framework for the accountability of that aid, i.e. we give it to you because your need is greater, but we will continue to give it only if you perform or make the effort we suggest. Moreover, the resulting 'double-bind' requirement (ultimately on local aid managers) to service local need but also account to the donor through a demonstration of effort or results sometimes conflicts with the accountability those civil and public servants have to their public (as discussed in Chapter 3).

Procedural justice Procedural justice means perceived fairness in how the rules are followed. By definition, then, it is relevant to corruption. Procedural justice has at least two main facets. First, there is fairness in terms of inclusion. Here, people ask themselves, 'Does our group have a say, a voice, in what decisions are taken, in the decision-making process?' Poverty Reduction Strategy Papers (PRSPs), which (theoretically) seek to promote ownership and partnership, should be procedurally just so that they promote inclusion. Second, there is fairness in terms of probity. Here, people ask themselves, 'Were the correct procedures followed, the existing rules respected?' If the perception is that they were not, a procedural injustice is born.

Procedures are relative. One person's 'wantok' system (pronounced 'one talk', entailing looking after one's family first) is another's nepotism. While donors might see the wantok system as nepotism and corruption, locals can see (if they choose to) loyalty, respect, leadership and, naturally enough, economic pragmatism. Each perspective, wantokism and nepotism, could be seen as a legitimating myth (Chapter 3). The problem, of course, is that the myths end up in conflict. Wantokism and nepotism, two ways of looking at the same behaviour, do not mix; that's the bad news. But there is good news, too. Among wantoks and advisers alike, there is a shared idea, a common goal; an identical purpose: the restoration of justice.

Let us pause for a moment just to clarify that we do not wish to overlook the reality of sheer greed and selfish opportunism, which surely exist in all societies. It is also important to understand, however, just when behaviour that might be interpreted as such, in fact, fits into a broader pattern of behaviour suggesting that something different, or perhaps something in addition, is going on. For example, a church minister told of his great difficulty in finding someone to be the treasurer of the church that he presided over in Malawi. In fact, he had sacked two previous incumbents because of 'corruption'. When he then asked for volunteers, nobody came forth, despite repeated pleading, and despite it being a respected position with high status in the community. He privately approached one man who he felt had always demonstrated great honesty and integrity and asked whether he would be treasurer. Even after considerable cajoling the man refused to take the position. Finally he declared, 'I couldn't have charge over such amounts of money and have my family go hungry.' He feared that his social (perhaps moral) obligations would undermine his 'integrity', and reasoned that it was better not to put himself in the difficult situation ... and let his family go hungry. That *is* integrity. So, yes, there is greed and corruption, but sometimes there may be something else going on – the human dynamics of dominance, justice and/or identity may be in play. When that is so, understanding the 'something else' may be a key to making aid projects work.

Interactional justice This type of justice is more closely tied than its predecessors to individual relations. Interactional justice is about being treated with respect. It has two major forms, informational and interpersonal. Informational justice means that individuals are informed about the procedures that are applied around them, and why. It is about being kept in the picture, being given some explanation, accorded a perspective. Interpersonal justice, by comparison, is more about personal treatment – for example, being treated with manners, not being spoken down to, etc. Common sources of interpersonal injustice are the workplace supervisor, authorities and third parties generally (Colquitt et al. 2001).

Stereotyping a threat can become a self-fulfilling prophecy. An expatriate adviser who implicitly sees local government as nepotistic and corrupt can inadvertently communicate that stereotype to local officials (known as 'non-verbal leakage'). This is more than just seeing what you expect to see; it is actually about producing in others the reactions that you expect, even when those reactions may not be characteristic of the people you are interacting with. If, for instance, one expects an indifferent response from teachers on a training course, then one's cursory delivery of the course might produce just that response – because others 'read' this expectation into one's own behaviour (MacLachlan 1993b). In the process, one unintentionally perhaps fuels the very stereotype itself. The resulting informational and interpersonal injustices can combine to motivate further coping behaviour. But we need to be careful about calling it merely corruption, or moonlighting.

Functionality

What justice theory enables us to do is to look at moonlighting behaviour, and wider issues of governance, as functional rather than dysfunctional, elevated rather than necessarily base. Moonlighting can represent an attempt to restore distributive justice; in fact so can switching to project aid, if one believes that this allows aid to be delivered directly to the poor, rather than through corrupt governments. Reducing one's radius of trust is a way of coping with an uncertain and unjust environment, for country and donor officials alike. Baulking at stereotypes is a way of reasserting one's own (and group's) place in the local system. Justice is not the only motive. But our point, and the point made by justice theory, is that restorative justice motives, processes and outcomes are often overlooked, even though they may really matter.

From justice to productivity

We have considered different forms of justice in the workplace because the different forms have different effects on work performance. Justice is not all 'hearts and flowers'. Perceptions of justice, or rather injustice, have demonstrated links to workplace motivation, job satisfaction and performance and commitment, including turnover intentions (Greenberg 2008). For example, distributive injustices are linked to work withdrawal, and procedural injustices are linked to poor work commitment and poor job performance (Colquitt et al. 2001). Commitment is the inverse of 'counterproductive work behaviours', such as theft, misappropriation and sabotage. These have been linked to procedural injustice directly (Cohen-Charash and Spector 2001). Distributive justice is linked to performance too, but relatively indirectly: 'When outcomes are distributed unfairly, people [first] examine the procedure ... to see if it was fair, and only if it is not do they withhold performance ...' (ibid.: 304).

Interactional justice also has links to performance and to job satisfaction. In a recent study of health workers in Malawi (McAuliffe et al. 2009a), we demonstrated clear links between interactional justice and job satisfaction. Figure 4.1 below shows how perceptions of justice or fairness co-varied with job satisfaction, with mean scores for the eight aspects of 'managerial consideration' plotted against degree of job satisfaction. The increasing mean scores moving from 'very dissatisfied' to 'very satisfied' show evidence of a positive relationship between perceived justice and reported levels of job satisfaction for almost all items on a justice scale. The more considerate the health workers believe their manager/supervisor is, the more they are likely to be satisfied in their job. The rise in the graph for almost all job satisfaction items indicates that how they were treated by their manager played a critical role in the degree of dissatisfaction workers reportedly experienced.

Distributive justice is often associated with perceptions of fair outcome for fair effort or input. An interesting finding from this study, however, is that when distributive justice is measured in terms

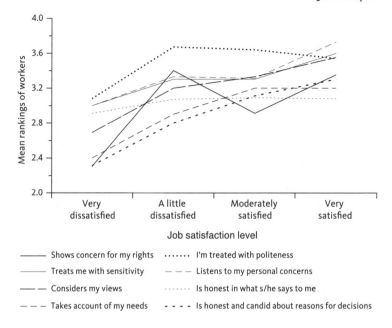

FIGURE 4.1 Relationship between job satisfaction and managerial consideration *Source*: McAuliffe et al. (2009a)

of fair outcome for these health workers in comparison with others doing similar work, the effect is heightened. Comparing the different elements of distributive justice yielded additional information that helped explain job satisfaction. Figure 4.2 plots the mean scores on satisfaction with pay, promotion and current assignments against responses on the job satisfaction scale (very dissatisfied to very satisfied). Satisfaction with the job was positively correlated with satisfaction with pay, promotion and current assignments, with the latter being more strongly correlated with job satisfaction than the other two items. These findings suggest that distributive injustice has a multiplicity of effects and, possibly, also indicate the danger of simply assuming that distributive injustice can be solved with a pay rise.

Procedural injustice and distributive injustice have each been linked, directly, to psychological distress (Tepper 2001). Whatever the specific source of the distress, however, it is likely to be highly unwelcome under the kinds of working conditions typically found

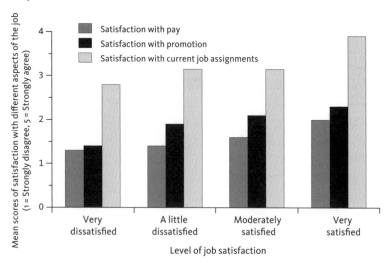

FIGURE 4.2 Degree of job satisfaction related to satisfaction with different aspects of the job *Source*: McAuliffe et al. (2009a)

in many low-income, civil service and aid work settings. As Ferrinho and van Lerberghe point out (2002), working in the civil service in low-income settings is certainly 'no picnic'. In an ongoing study one of us conducted with health workers in Tanzania and Malawi (see McAuliffe et al. 2009c), we found evidence of tiredness and burnout due to injustice in the distribution of workloads. This is also evident from the following quote from one clinical officer in Tanzania.

> I saw that I am being oppressed. I have been giving service more than usual. I am saying that we have to use brain very much in our work, concentration. You cannot concentrate as you are required if you have a very big number of patients to attend to. Everybody needs your service; therefore, we become very tired. You work beyond your capacity. We are serving very many people in a day than before when our colleagues were around. We used to share patients. At the moment our colleagues have left, at times we are told to sell our day off. You are told to come to work and then they will pay you. This is because patients are many and doctors are few. In spite of your time to rest you have to come to work so as to reduce the number of patients.

Feelings of injustice are signals to do something about the situation. They signal a need to adapt, cope with a threat of some kind. In our findings this manifests itself in health workers who plan to leave their posts, as illustrated by the following quote from a nurse midwife in Tanzania: 'I will go and I do not need to deceive you, I will go. Maybe if they will improve the work environment and increase number of workers and our rights to be brought to these villages. But if they will continue to deny us all these things I will leave.'

Specifically, feelings of injustice signal issues with one's status. Individuals, at least, 'use justice perceptions to infer their social standing within the group' (Barsky and Kaplan 2007: 292). One participant in our study cried with frustration at not having her status recognized:

> I was medical attendant, and ... I went to school, studied and finished in 2008, I then started working, but, up to this moment, I haven't been promoted, I mean my cadre hasn't been changed, I am still called medical attendant, and I am receiving medical attendant salary ... I am a nurse and I am working as a nurse, the salary I am receiving is attendants' salary ... the working morale is starting to decline [crying].

Presumably the causal link can go the other way, from social standing to perceived injustice. Whatever the directionality, however, status means hierarchy and thus dominance (Chapter 3). Justice and dominance are thereby linked. We return to this in detail in Chapter 5. For the moment, however, let us consider that perceptions of distributive injustice can prime a search for shortfalls in procedure. Donors may sense inequity in a government's or an NGO's distribution of resources: distributive injustice. This prompts a search for procedural irregularities. Among locals, moonlighting spreads. If a colleague is moonlighting and getting away with it this may be perceived as procedural injustice; he or she is seen as exempted from the rules that apply to the rest of the staff. Moonlighting begets moonlighting. Coping strategies can be adaptive for the individual and immediate group, although possibly less so for an entire institution and the wider public it serves. The bad news in all this is the misunderstanding that different perspectives, and belief systems, can engender. The good news is that there is more, much more, to corruption than meets the eye. Much of it is, potentially, actually quite positive. Many of the behaviours, stories and stereotypes are motivated not merely by personal or group gain. Beneath the conflict is a shared touchstone, a shared goal: restoring justice. Having considered a taxonomy of justice, summarized in Table 4.1, we now think through how it applies to particular situations in international aid.

Interventions

Having recognized the importance of justice motivation, we now have a more solid basis for possible interventions. We have seen, for instance, that discrepant perspectives propagate miscommunication and conflict. Shared goals, we also know, are a key way of bringing conflicting groups back together, into alignment and harmony (Carr 2003). For such initiatives to work, reviews indicate, the goals need to be first and foremost shared (termed 'superordinate'), they need to be attainable, and they need to be sequential, not singular. There need to be several, in succession, if change is to be sustained (ibid.).

Project aid

We have not forgotten that there is an alternative to direct budget support. Is project aid any less susceptible to justice concerns than budget support?

Project ADDUP is an acronym for 'Are Development Discrepancies Undermining Performance?' The 'discrepancies' at stake are those extant differences in working conditions between project workers, whose point of origin is local, versus expatriates. ADDUP's focus is pecuniary – on those differences the professor scorned us for missing earlier on. Such gaps in income, we have seen, can be symbolic as much as economic. They symbolize distributive, procedural and interactional injustice. It is not uncommon, for instance, for expatriate/local pay ratios, across groups, individuals and institutions, to exceed 10:1. Most of us would find such discrepancies awkward, to say the least. Certainly they are not conducive to the kind of teamwork that capacity development, hopefully mutual in its direction, requires.

ADDUP, funded by the United Kingdom's Economic and Social Research Council and the Department for International Development, aims to bring the question of pay discrepancy out into the open. The project was also conceived to explore the relevance of work justice theory and motive, and to addressing the issue in practical terms. Our starting point for that practical focus is, once again, functional versus dysfunctional coping strategies.

Coping strategies

A process-based account of what coping strategies may be employed, and how they function or malfunction, is summarized in Figure 4.3. This figure builds on an earlier one described by MacLachlan and Carr (2005) but incorporates some of the results from the ADDUP project (2009). The process begins with a pay comparison ('equity comparison').

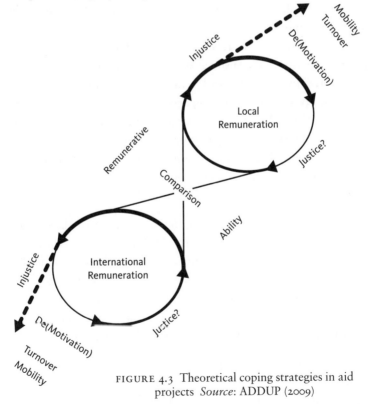

FIGURE 4.3 Theoretical coping strategies in aid projects *Source*: ADDUP (2009)

For an expatriate, on sharply higher remuneration compared to a local counterpart, perceived distributive injustice may spark some discomfort. That is quite likely perhaps if, as social dominance and justice theories predict, people are initially drawn into aid work through a social conscience (and hierarchy attenuation motivation). Such discomfort may fuel the sense of culture shock and turnover intention that many expatriates, at least on first assignment, feel. Justice restoration theory predicts that groups and individuals will work harder to restore a sense of fair play ('I get paid more, but I work harder'). The problem with this strategy is that it is not sustainable. No one can consistently work ten times harder than anyone else, at least not without burning out prematurely. Hence the worker may start to convince themselves psychologically that they are somehow a better worker; that they do not need to work as hard as their local and lesser-paid counterparts in order to achieve the same result. This is an insidious process; it takes time. The net result, however, is lowered productivity. Alternatively, they may take the view that they are somehow more knowledgeable or have greater expertise – the ensuing result is a slowdown in work input (a demotivation), coupled with reinforced dominance.

For the local worker, pay comparison is liable to fuel a perception of distributive injustice, both in terms of inequity (many locals are as well qualified as their expatriate counterparts, at times better) and need (many local workers have a more extended network of dependants than their expatriate counterparts), as evidenced by the following quote from a medical officer in Tanzania:

> The problems affect my working efficiency because you have done the work and you are not paid. This leads to psychological effects and feelings that you are not given your right … you find yourself wasting much time on solving them instead of doing the work … As we all know, in Africa we have extended families, there are many people depending on you so when you are not paid your salary it affects you psychologically and your family too.

Theories of restorative processes predict that workers will try to restore a sense of balance (Carr et al. 1998). The most obvious and perhaps practicable way to do so is to withdraw one's input to match one's (reduced) outcomes. Hence the theory predicts a second demotivation and, overall, a *double* demotivation – on behalf of both the expatriate (above) and the local worker.

As Figure 4.3 shows, what one party does will affect how the other reacts, and vice versa. For example, any withdrawal or counterproductive behaviours by the local counterpart may reinforce the expatriate's sense of superiority ('I am paid more, maybe I am worth more'). Similarly, when the expatriate needs some help from his or her local counterpart, then the hand of friendship may be somewhat less forthcoming ('you're the expert, you solve the problem!').

To sum up, Figure 4.3 suggests that in higher-paid expatriate workers we might see a combination of awkwardness/guilt plus superiority. Among the lower-paid country nationals, we might see a combination of indignation and withdrawal. In short, we might detect a double demotivation.

Table 4.2 contains the key results of an organizational survey conducted at the National University of Malawi, with aid-funded and locally salaried lecturers. The table reports statistically significant differences between the different pay groups, and individuals

TABLE 4.2 Items on which pay groups differed

	Expatriates	Nationals
Items about foreign expatriates		
Some expatriates on large salaries feel guilty because they earn more than local workers	3.4	2.0
Expatriates are better employees than their local counterparts	2.7	1.6
Items about host instructors		
Expatriates who work abroad should work under the same terms and conditions as local people	2.2	4.1
Most companies are unfair to their local employees	3.3	4.6
Local people are demotivated by the large salaries that some expatriates earn	2.9	4.2

Note: Scale ranged from 1 to 5, higher ratings = stronger agreement
Source: MacLachlan and Carr (2005)

in them. It is clear from Table 4.2 that the central tendency among the expatriates is to agree with the item about expatriate guilt. Their local counterparts, however, do not detect this feeling, since they clearly disagree that any guilt is being felt. This is a missed communication. Expatriates tend to be equivocal about whether they are superior to their local colleagues. The mean value does reflect the fact that many would agree rather than disagree, however, and any attempts to disguise the truth would probably work to suppress the true rating, not inflate it. In addition, the local workers clearly disagree with their expatriate counterparts about inherent ability and motivation. Our estimate is therefore that there is some underlying sense of superiority being reflected among this particular sample of expatriate workers, along with the guilt (Demotivation 1).

Table 4.2 also gives some figures for the average response to direct items about equity, fairness and demotivation. Once again the local and expatriate workers significantly disagree. Locals feel strongly that terms and conditions should be equivalent, or equal. Expatriates disagree. Locals feel strongly that companies, as well as educational sector groups, are behaving unfairly, whereas expatriates are equivocal, and local workers agree that local people are demotivated by the salaries that some expatriates earn. Again there is a miscommunication here, since expatriates themselves do not detect the depth of demotivation that locals report. Overall, therefore, we estimate that there is a second demotivation going on, with local workers demoralized and expatriate workers failing to pick up on the psychology of their colleagues (Demotivation 2).

As a whole, Table 4.2 reflects a wider pattern of demotivation resulting from the justice motive. Extreme pay differentials prompt feelings of injustice, which is distressing for workers. In order to cope with such differentials, the pay groups may resort to 'othering' and sometimes divisive coping strategies. These strategies range from delusions of importance, i.e. social dominance, through to anger and withdrawal. Such reactions would not be incompatible with the kinds of reaction we saw in health service sectors (above). To that extent, justice motives cast as much light on project aid as they do on moonlighting and corruption in government institutions.

The data from Table 4.2 were from just one survey in one organ-

> ### Box 4.1 Indicative quotes from qualitative research in the Solomon Islands
>
> A local perspective
>
> 'Australians are coming in with a higher and higher and better lifestyle, making a lot of money ... what [they] might get in one week is what Solomon Islanders might live on in a year ... that's just sure to engender some bitterness eventually' Solomon Islands church leader, 2005
>
> An expatriate perspective
>
> 'I was introduced to your [ADDUP Project] work recently during a visit to the Solomon Islands, when an AusAID employee was talking about her experiences in this location, in particular her guilt regarding the gulf that exists between herself and the local islanders' Senior staff Counselling in Aid sector, March 2006
>
> *Source*: ADDUP seminar series, preliminary site visits (2007)

ization in one country. Project ADDUP, however, is currently expanding the 'test bed' for possible motivational consequences of extreme pay diversity. The project adopts a multi-sector approach (health, education and business), and cluster samples not only from land-locked economies (Malawi, Uganda), but also from both transition economies (China, India) and island nations (Papua New Guinea and the Solomon Islands). The emerging findings are broadly supportive of the model described above.

Anecdotal site reports from Phase I of ADDUP suggest that pay discrepancies, and their potential to undermine aid and development initiatives, are not confined to one particular site or sector. Box 4.1 contains a sample of the kinds of sentiment that the topic of pay differences can engender. The comments come from the South Pacific region, and refer to an aid project there. It is funded principally by two particular national aid agencies, from Australia and New Zealand. As the box reveals, the differences in work pay and conditions have the potential to undermine the laudable goals in the programme itself, a suggestion indirectly being tested by the emerging results of Project ADDUP's multi-country study (see Carr et al., forthcoming).

Interventions

What practical use is justice theory to project aid? A clue lies in the perspectives of expatriates salaried locally. In our study, they comprised a third pay group, who were technically working for the Malawian government, on local salaries alongside local lecturers. With their expatriate colleagues, however, they also shared some cultural background. Hence they had a proverbial foot in each camp: socio-economic parity (or similarity) with their local counterparts; and relative sociocultural similarity with their fellow expatriates. Such part-alignments raise an intriguing question: whose view of the situation do they share? Was their perspective most closely positioned economically, with the locals, or culturally, with expatriates?

Fascinatingly, we observed a bit of both. Expatriates on local salaries and conditions realized that higher-paid expatriates did feel some guilt. Their ratings on the guilt item in Table 4.2 did not differ from those of the expatriates on higher pay. In addition to this, however, the expatriates on local pay also understood better that local staff were demotivated. Their ratings did *not* differ significantly from those of their local colleagues on the demotivation item. Overall, therefore, expatriates whose pay and conditions matched the local conditions, and whose cultural background was closer to that of expatriates generally, may have been relatively well positioned, compared to their higher-paid counterparts, to share perspectives.

Perhaps we can accept that perspective-sharing is important for teamwork and capacity development, as well as for breakdowns in communication and barriers to such goals. If so, the findings for expatriate local pay suggest one way forward. That way forward can be broken down into three interrelated pathways: group, institutional and individual.

Groups In the previous chapter, we learned how pre-departure training, if it is conducted at all, focuses on sociocultural not socio-economic diversity, and on preparing the expatriate for the sojourn, not the host. The findings of our study in Malawi, and more latterly the ongoing ADDUP initiative, are suggesting an additional focus: mutual group preparation (pre-departure, plus post-arrival) on how to manage socio-economic diversity. Existing knowledge of organizational behaviour contains a range of techniques for closing the gaps in expectation and communication. These include, for instance, much more realistic job previews (broaching the taboo); asking each group to estimate the justice perceptions of the other and then swapping them over to expose the gaps (the Selmer technique); and work sample tests that role-play how to handle objections such as those listed in Table 4.2 and Box 4.1.

Evidence from our locally salaried aid workers, for instance, suggested that realigning the salary gap, even partly, might help close the communication gap. In aid work today, there has been a continuing expansion in the role played by non-governmental organizations (NGOs). NGOs tend to pay less than their governmental, consultancy-focused and multilateral agency counterparts (Werker and Ahmed 2008). Aid and development work is increasingly outsourced to them, in part because they are efficient, competitive and professionally managed. According to Werker and Ahmed's review, their competitive salary bands have not impacted on the quality of their recruits, who are often highly qualified and intrinsically motivated. NGOs may also be good candidates for competition- and efficiency-promoting NGO voucher systems, for consumers of NGO services (Easterly 2006: ch. 2). Hence strengthening reliance on NGOs, and NGO salary structures, offers one potential countermeasure against double demotivation. As we will see in Chapter 5, however, NGOs and civil society are no magic bullet; in fact, some even cast them as integral to many of the difficulties with international aid.

Locally, a range of interventions are possible, too. During the initial site visit by ADDUP to Papua New Guinea (PNG), for instance, we were reminded again (as in the studies of governance) that the differences are not simply about money. It is the symbolic value or function of money, and pay, which is at stake. Lower pay signals lower respect, lower value in the system, and social dominance. These relationship factors create barriers between aid workers, nicely encapsulated in a local phrase, colloquially used to describe PNG's official 'dual pay' policy: 'economic apartheid'. Symbolic actions are able to counteract such perceptions, by signalling that the staff members are valued (interactional justice). Similarly, in our research with health workers, management support and being listened to by managers were stronger predictors of commitment than pay alone.

Institutions Organizational interventions often need to work hand in hand with interventions at the institutional level. In PNG, for instance, the concept of dual salary (for local versus expatriate workers) is not only a line-management issue for organizations, it is a policy left over from colonial and post-colonial days when capacity was relatively low. The policy aspect of pay differences is a reminder that it is not enough to be tackling pay differences at any one level alone. Double demotivation must be addressed in institutions as well as in organizations, using ADDUP data to lobby government.

Among the most prominent of institutions in aid and development is the Paris Declaration on Aid Effectiveness (www.gc21.de/ibt/alumni/ibt/docs/Paris_Declaration_en.pdf). The declaration lists a set of principles for aid and development work, among which the most frequently cited are (i) Alignment and (ii) Harmonization. Basically, alignment means respecting the views and perceptions of national governments. In comparison, harmonization is essentially ensuring that the providers of aid are singing from the same song sheet, i.e. that there is minimal inter-agency duplication and conflict.

Within the context of the Paris Declaration the varied salaries and wide pay differences (both between agencies and between expatriates and nationals) may be problematic, and we have found that open discussion of them is quite often taboo. They are the 'elephant in the aid parlour'. For instance, not one expatriate attended our ADDUP project dissemination workshops in Uganda or Malawi, despite invitations to do so, and to participate in the research that was being disseminated. Project ADDUP touches a nerve. Pay reflects status. ADDUP challenges myths about meritocracy, reciprocity and social equity. Questioning such myths is taboo. There will be resistance, but hopefully change.

Conclusion

Perceptions of justice, and injustice, signal one's place in a hierarchy. If injustices are allowed to persist, in a field that claims to reduce them, a spirit of contradiction will prevail. Aid workers, like organizations and institutions, will become cynical. It is behaviourally naive to expect discrepant incentives systems not to have a negative impact on the work that aid organizations, institutions and individuals do! It's the contradiction, stupid! Burying our heads in the sand of 'regional labour markets', or 'Pareto efficiency' (Chapter 2), simply won't work. Making aid more effective depends on building work relationships that are just.

Beyond restoring justice, what happens next? Injustice is stressful and potentially debilitating; we have seen that. But once assuaged, feelings of justice will possibly fade. In the same way that a visit to the dentist, although dreaded, will remove a toothache and enable you to face the day ahead, a satisfied need is not a motivator. It simply enables us to concentrate on the job at hand. New needs will arise to take the place of the original. In that sense, all the research and thinking about workplace justice is actually about injustice, and how to remove it from the field of concern.

What comes next is the big question. What human dynamics move a person, group or institution to engage with others, and with the job at hand? In the next chapter, we argue that those motivators include identity – specifically a sense of pride in, and respect for, who we are, and what we can do.

5 | Identity

'We want health, housing, and education. But not at the expense of losing our own soul, our own identity, a say in our lives. We refuse to sacrifice the essence of what makes us Aboriginal people' Dodson (1998: 8)

'Let us think for a moment of the expatriate relief worker arriving for his morning clinic at the refugee camp. The cloud of approaching dust announces the arrival of the Landrover, with our relief worker, the sole occupant, at the wheel. He doesn't know it, but he's not alone. With him he brings cross-cultural transference and counter-transference: In the back of his Landrover are White Colonial Masters, Euro-centrism, parentalism, professionalism, reductionism, capitalism, and other "isms", which he, and I, are simply unaware of. The point is, no matter his intentions, he is a symbol. Even if he does not embody that which he symbolizes to others, he is never himself alone' MacLachlan (2002: 242, translated from German)

'Contrary to conventional stereotypes, the aid agencies themselves are as much supplicants as the countries they support. There are predictable effects on the relationships between the aid offices within recipient countries: rivalry, duplication and overlap, and competition for prominence in some very crowded fields' Moore (2007: 42)

The context for Pat Dodson's public address cited above was and still is welfare/aid dependency. In that context, maintaining a strong sense of identity is crucial for ongoing development. Yet aid systems can work to undermine that very capacity. They can foster dependency, sapping individuals' confidence in who they are and what they stand for, their uniqueness. Every gift, it seems, takes something away. The second and third quotes make a similar point. In these cases too, one identity can impinge on another, through the conduit of aid workers. Both examples link identity to culture. In this case, however, it is the aid workers whose identity is problematic, through the cultural assumptions they bring to work. This chapter asks: how often does aid work divest the 'aided' of their sense of 'who they are', and in that sense undermine its own rhetoric?

Soul wounds

Let us take a dramatic example of identity in action, in a development-related context, and then try to understand it. Marin (1998) has described how a traditional indigenous group in Colombia, the U'wa (which means intelligent people who know how to speak), responded to planned oil exploration in their traditional lands. They stated that should the plans go ahead they would collectively commit suicide; to be cut off from their ancestral site, to be removed from their stories passed down from generation to generation, would be the same as being killed as a people, in fact a fate worse than death. In their own words the U'wa say: 'We must care for, not maltreat, because for us it is forbidden to kill with knives, machetes or bullets. Our weapons are thought, the word, our power is wisdom; we prefer death before seeing our sacred ancestors profaned' (Jackson 2002: 97).

What these words indicate is that identity is so central and fundamental to a people's sense of being that it may be worth dying for. In the above case it is being suggested that, collectively, it *is* worth dying for. Not because the U'wa's lives are explicitly physically under threat (say, through violence or starvation), but rather because the lives they lead are under threat psychologically. The value of what they stand for, and what stands for them, is being challenged. To put it another way, this time with an expression from an indigenous cultural island group in the Pacific, cultures with a history of colonialism have been left, even today, with deep and enduring scars on their identity, termed 'soul wounds' (Rapadas 2007).

Evocative metaphors like these imply that culture enables us to face life and avoid death, or at least thoughts of death. Cottoning on to this, although basing their work largely on the interdisciplinary writings of Ernest Becker, a trio of psychologists has led a new line of experimental research into fundamental existential issues. These are issues like 'Who am I?', 'What's the meaning of life?' and 'What will happen to me when I die?' (Pyszczysnki et al. 2003). A review of Becker's work and the research supporting what the three researchers have described as Terror Management Theory is beyond the scope of this book. The central premise in Terror Management Theory, however, is that our concerns about mortality – our death – play a pervasive and far-reaching role in our daily lives. The human capacity for self-reflection, and our ability to anticipate the future, allows us to contemplate the rather gloomy inevitability of our own demise. Because of that we have evolved, over eons of human history, elaborate and adaptive ways of self-protection. These include cultural beliefs, and belief systems.

Along with Sigmund Freud and Otto Rank, Becker believed that humans would be frozen in inaction and abject terror if they were continually to contemplate their vulnerability and mortality. Thus cultural world-views evolved, and these were socially constructed beliefs about reality, which were socially shared by groups of people. These beliefs helped, at least in part, to cope with and to that extent manage the terror engendered by the fact that we know we are going to die one day. The way in which reality is constructed through these cultural world-views helps to manage the fear of death by supplying coherent, internally consistent, meaningful answers to our own mortality. In fact, social psychologists have long contended that societal norms are socially constructed in part to build meaning into life, and by implication death (Sherif 1936; Festinger 1950). Such needs are arguably in part why living in cultures very different to our own brings on 'culture shock' (Furnham and Bochner 1986). Although far less enduring, culture shock, like soul wounds, challenges core life defences.

In a sense, then, cultures give people a role to play, distracting them from the anxiety of worrying about what they fear most. Cultures provide recipes for immortality, either symbolically (such as amassing great fortunes that out-survive their originator), or spiritually (such as going to heaven). So following the rules and interpretations of your culture – cultivating your role in society – can ensure a form of immortality. But it also has an equally important function in the here-and-now: the idea that each of us is a valuable entity, in a universe that has some meaning, is encouraged and supported. This helps us to build and maintain a semblance of self-esteem. Indeed, self-esteem in itself becomes a primary psychological 'defence mechanism', through which culture serves a death-denying function.

The U'wa may more fully appreciate the life-saving and death-denying function of culture than do others in financially wealthier economies. Sometimes people can find themselves, and protect themselves, through a collective identity shared by others. As Isaiah Berlin states in *Two Concepts of Liberty*, 'When I am among my own people, they understand me, as I understand them; and this understanding creates within me a sense of being somebody in the world' (1958: 43). Viewed in this way, culture becomes a mainstay not only of sanity, but also of living a meaningful, and purposeful, life. Fundamentally, then, anything that challenges culture may engender a serious reaction (Smyth et al. 2003). In the next section, we describe some of the often subtle ways in which international aid might be one such challenge.

Group identity

The opening quotations are reminders that individuals live within groups, but that groups also live within individuals. Belonging to a group may be a fundamental building block in one's identity, the sense of 'who one is in the world'. Identity is fundamentally a group process. Group-based theories of identity focus on two main ideas, social comparison and self-esteem. Their argument is that all human beings need to belong to a set of groups, and that they frequently change their modus operandi ('MO') from individual to group entity and vice versa (Carr 2004). The extent to which people from different societies do this, and in which mode they spend more time, varies considerably. Writing from an African perspective, for instance, Bandawe (2005) has suggested that a common theme which pervades many of Africa's different cultures, and distinguishes them from other cultures, is a notion called *uMunthu*. The precise term differs from place to place – for instance, in South Africa it is *uBunthu*. In Chichewa (one of the Malawian languages), the philosophy is conveyed through a phrase, 'Umuntu ngumuntu ngabantu' ('a person is a person through other persons'). Wherever the concept appears, however, the sense of self is dependent on identity, and on belongingness with a group or groups.

There may be a contrast here with notions about identity that others bring with them from elsewhere. *UMunthu* is very different, for instance, from the individualism enshrined in Descartes' *cogito ergo sum*. The credo 'I think, therefore I am' is a perspective that arguably pervades a range of cultural groups outside of Africa. If something as basic as the self is defined in radically different ways across these different settings, then we start to get a sense of how the expatriate relief worker depicted at the beginning of the chapter, however well meaning, might disturb a cultural host. *UMunthu* is a reminder that, even though he may see himself as an individual, to others he is a person through other persons – for example, the cultural group he represents, or those he interacts with. From a relatively individualistic perspective he may not fully appreciate the amount of group-based cultural baggage in the back of his four-wheel-drive. However helpful they may be in the short term, those cultural artefacts may eventually insinuate themselves into the indigenous culture, and its sense of unique identity, in counterproductive ways.

One of the ideas embedded in the above, and in the Paris Declaration on Aid Effectiveness, is the principle of Alignment – that donor organizations align their efforts with the priorities identified by the poorer countries. When left to decide their own pathway, a positive sense of identity can enable groups to do well. In laboratory tasks, for instance, groups that have pride in who they are have been found to be more motivated in what they do, to go the extra mile more often, and to be more productive (respectively, Glynn and Carr 1999; Van Knippenberg 2000; Worchel et al. 1998). Outside of the laboratory, group dynamics have been studied in women's work collectives, for example micro-credit networks in Nicaragua (V. Schein 1999, 2003). Even in adversity, these, according to the women, provide 'a sense of sisterhood and self-esteem' (Schein 1999: 108). Those in turn enable the businesses to develop and promote wider social and economic change (Schein 2003: 124). According to

Schein's review (ibid.), similar results have been found across a range of economies in Latin America (Guatemala, Honduras, Peru), as well as in Africa (Ghana, Tanzania). Central to each, however, is the motivating effect of belonging to a group about which individuals feel proud and efficacious.

Group identity goes farther. It can reportedly counter the effects of social dominance and injustice. In the words of one of Schein's interviewees from a labour union, for instance: 'Before, I let men mistreat me, but now I know how to defend myself' (2003: 136). From Schein's own observations, 'women gave examples of changes in their relationships with their husbands as a result of being a member of the group. They were able to alter the relationship so that it became more balanced and *egalitarian*' (ibid.: 136, emphasis added). As a result of such changes, according to Schein: 'women in several work-related groups described improvements in their housing, food supplies, and children's education' (ibid.: 138). Hence, in some circumstances there may exist a synergistic link between dominance, justice and identity, specifically identity in groups.

A second important idea embedded in the above example is that one identity can impinge on another – in effect becoming a significant impediment to group '*dignidad*' (dignity) (ibid.: 126). An example of 'how' such impediments can materialize is found in trauma counselling, as part of relief and development work. A cultural assumption in many relatively individualistic theories of counselling is that it is therapeutic to 'talk through' a traumatic experience. The rationale is that talking about it reduces the risk that the underlying effects of the trauma will remain inaccessible, perhaps becoming problematic and manifesting themselves in maladaptive behaviours or psychological problems. In at least one relief and development setting familiar to us, however, a different but equally valid form of coping emerged. Enabling it to surface was the employment of counsellors who were themselves former refugees. They found that traumatized victims wanted to forget what had happened, rather than 'raking over the coals' by 'talking it through' (Kanyangale and MacLachlan 1995). The preference was to get on with life in the most adaptive and perhaps pragmatic way possible, by 'forgetting' (or not repeatedly focusing on) the past. In this case, then, a 'foreign' form of assistance (trauma counselling) was repudiated in favour of techniques more closely aligned with local expectations and customs (see also Chapter 6). In group identity terms, one form of cultural assumption, quite possibly inappropriate and harmful, was prevented from impinging on another, as it could so easily have done.

Institutional identity

Institutions are collections of groups with a shared culture. The identity of these institutions can be described in various terms, such as 'governance', 'stability risk' and 'environment for business'. Features like these can be measured objectively, using official indicators such as how long it takes to set up a business, and subjectively – for instance, how much 'corruption' potential foreign investors perceive in the economy in question. Such features have been linked to 'development'. In emerging economies, for example, objective levels of governance have been linked to the amount of foreign direct investment (Ping-Ngoh Foo and Chein-Hsing Sung 2002). Executives seem to be more drawn towards investing in economies that they perceive, subjectively, to be more 'stable' (Festervand and Jones 2001). Stability seems to be a facet of so-called 'investor confidence', which often reflects the identity that a country's institutions are seen to have. Such reflections can be very powerful and consequential. Even a smidgen of investor confidence can provide much-needed resources for institutions to develop inside lower-income home economies. That process reportedly happened, for instance, in India in the late 1980s/early 1990s. The increase in confidence in the country and its institutions played a significant part in boosting internal confidence and subsequent economic growth (Basu 2007). Institutional identity, both projected and self-attributed, was crucial to economic development.

Individual identity

Increases in investor confidence, like the resources that follow them, can have consequences not only for the local institution and groups within it, but also for the individuals in those groups. For example, it is individuals who start businesses, take risks, work to develop an enterprise. Qualities like entrepreneurial orientation can and do make key differences to how well an enterprise venture succeeds or fails (Krauss et al. 2005). Some individuals will persist with entrepreneurial activity even in the most adverse of circumstances, a quality termed 'resilience' (Carr et al. 1997). At the same time, of course, these qualities may be constrained by their environment. Systems that deprive individuals of investor confidence, no matter how talented the individual may be, will halt the process (Singer 2008). For example, investors may fail to back a particular individual because of their caste, if they think that others will fail to do business with them. In the end the entrepreneur fails because of their perceived social identity, whatever their fundamental individual talent. Unfortunately, caste can become a self-fulfilling prophecy, as the more a group's members fail to achieve, the more the original scepticism that provoked it (among a majority group) is reinforced. Human factors like this – developmental barriers – are aptly called 'strong situations', precisely because there's not a lot that individual – or even group – identities can do about them.

US president Barack Obama grapples with this issue, as it relates to race, in his book *Dreams from My Father*: 'I had come to understand myself as a Black American, and was understood as such, that understanding remained unanchored to place' (Obama 2007: 139) and reaches the conclusion that the only way to prevent this self-fulfilling prophecy is to find a community: 'What I needed was a community that cut deeper than the common despair that black friends and I shared when reading the latest crime statistics ... a place where I could put down stakes and test my commitments' (ibid.: 139).

Economist Kaushik Basu (2007) has provided an analysis of how powerful these situations connected to identity can be. Basu's analysis focuses on the situation of 'participative equity', i.e. what we have called justice (Chapter 4). Basu argues that compared to injustice, justice boosts pride in one's identity, thereby enabling economic performance. Here again is a link between justice and identity. We agree and would go farther. We would add that the word 'equity' in Basu's term 'participative equity' is consistent with a role for social dominance: identity depends not only on restoring a sense of justice but also, more fundamentally perhaps, on shedding the sense of dominance. Next in this chapter, we explore how these three steps – dominance, justice and identity – can be 'cross-hatched' with other salient ideas. A model for that process is presented in Figure 5.1. The model reconfigures the triangular relationship we have described into a series of interlocking relationships that can also be imagined as 'stacking up' on top of each other.

The importance of relationships in aid work is becoming increasingly recognized (Eyben 2006), both in terms of relationships between government, UN agencies, NGOs and communities (e.g. Pasteur and Scott-Villiers 2006), and between donor and recipient (e.g. Eyben 2005). Indeed, aid workers themselves have identified relationship-building as the key factor in the success of capacity development initiatives (Girgis 2007; McWha, forthcoming), and attempts are now being made to measure the value of these relationships (McWha and MacLachlan, forthcoming). Here, however, we want to stress the importance of sensitively navigating such relationships for strengthening positive identity and thus real social, as well as economic, 'development'. We want to illustrate that development, as we see it, is a relational term – about relationships between people – rather than a purely economic term (recall our argument in Chapter 1). Thus we will use examples both from low-income countries and also from the Aboriginal peoples of (relatively high-average-income) Australia to drive home this point.

In his ground-breaking book *Development as Freedom* (1999), Amartya Sen equates development with the freedom to realize one's potential and the capacity to make choices utilizing that potential. In that regard, we want to use Figure 5.1 to help us think through how groups, individuals and institutions may interact with one another, from differing positions in a social hierarchy, and to apply these to the context of international aid. Groups are often locked in a struggle for 'identity', or what Tajfel (1978) termed a social identity that is 'positively distinctive'. The model underlines the fact that identity is socially defined and constructed: it always involves the actual or symbolic presence of others. Of course, as we saw in Chapter 3, and in Figure 5.1, the groups are not evenly placed. There is an 'upper' and a 'lower' rung. The fundamental 'problematic' in mutual identity development lies not with the lower but rather with the upper layer: it is they who need to adjust, in order for justice, identity and ultimately perhaps 'development' to be mutually enabled. As we have seen above, strong positions are often made from 'other' as well as 'own' identities.

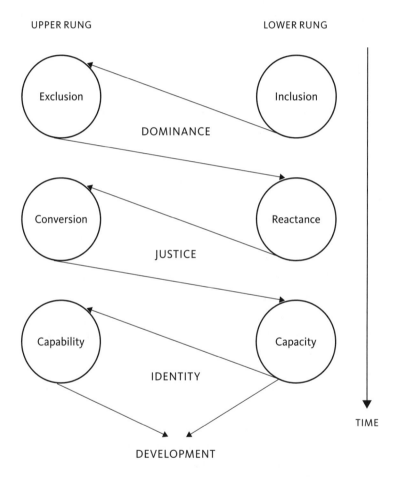

Note: These are relatively broad, recurring forms of positioning only. They are not rigidly programmed dispositions, nor sets of dispositions

FIGURE 5.1 Navigating the dynamics of aid and development
Source: Adapted from Carr (2004)

Inclusion

It makes sense that minority groups should often try to bring about their own inclusion in majority society. For example, when arriving in a new country to which they have chosen to emigrate, immigrants may attempt to try on aspects of their chosen host culture (Horgan 2000). Or a minority or disempowered group may find some comparative 'refuge' in at least some of the majority or more empowered groups' customs and beliefs. At other times, they may be less likely to embrace the other culture – for example, where there are present or past elements of slavery, and continued racial oppression (MacLachlan 2006). These less positive aspects may result in a socially disadvantaged group incorporating at least some of their lower status into their own view of themselves – their own identity. In his autobiography, Malcolm X describes how African-Americans would apply skin lighteners in an attempt to assimilate themselves with the whiter majority (Haley and Malcolm X 2001). After the British proclaimed what we now term Australia *'terra nullus'* ('empty land'), successive generations of oppression meant that the policy almost became reality and the indigenous people lost much of their previously esteemed identity (MacLachlan 2006).

Assimilation, of course, can take more subtle and everyday forms. In organizational mergers and takeovers, for instance, employees from the less powerful firm may attempt to embrace elements in, and join the culture of, the more powerful entity (Carr 2004). Analogous processes may take place in post-colonial organizations. Aid frequently entails bilateral projects, for instance, while international joint ventures may involve a wealthier 'partner' manufacturing goods or services in a middle-income transition setting. In these projects, individuals are recruited from the local community and local organizations are attached to the project itself. Often enough, perhaps, 'As in a relationship between landlord and tenant, at the centre of the donor–recipient relationship is an exchange of deference and compliance by the client in return for the patron's provision' (Crewe and Harrison 1998: 11). The less empowered group may be assimilated into the schemes of the more empowered group.

A key point about assimilation is that it is often motivated by a desire to join the majority group, to be included, even perhaps at the expense of one's minority background. From Figure 5.1 we see that attempts at inclusion may be met with resistance. Thus dominant host groups in a society that supposedly 'welcomes' new immigrants from lower-income countries may also resist them (Berry, forthcoming; Hernandez et al., forthcoming): skilled migrants from many lower-income countries experience employment discrimination, even though they may be equally strong as job applicants as their counterpart migrants from wealthier economies (Carr and Coates 2003). Indeed, the harder an individual or minority group pushes to be accepted, the more they may be seen to pose a threat to majority privilege, and hence the greater is the rebuff (Moscovici 1976). Reactions like that, we have seen from Chapter 3, are the dynamics of dominance.

Exclusion

In time, Figure 5.1 suggests, repeated assertions of dominance will start to have an effect. Repeatedly being treated as a second-class citizen is not without some psychological consequences for the oppressed. Eventually it may even undermine basic self-confidence, and thereby identity itself. Writers from a range of disciplines and perspectives have written about these effects, longer-term, as regards colonization. For example, the psychiatrist and social activist Frantz Fanon describes how stereotypes can meddle with identity so much that the minority group ends up having 'Black skins [but] White masks' (1961). Once internalized, these stereotypes have the potential to become self-fulfilling. They achieve that dubious distinction by insidiously undermining performance, to such an extent that the label 'second-class' appears to fit even to the wearer.

A telling story about this process appears in Hoff and Pandey (2004). These researchers, based at the World Bank, were struck by a seeming passivity among villagers faced with high teacher absenteeism in their village schools. The researchers undertook an experimental study of inequities produced by the Indian caste system. This was in the rural areas of Uttar Pradesh, one of the poorest areas of India. They wanted to examine the impact of caste on individuals' self-confidence and expectations, so they asked Hindu high-caste (Thakur, Brahmin and Vaishya) and low-caste

(Chamar, actually 'untouchable') boys from a junior high school to solve as many maze problems as they could from a packet of such problems. As an incentive for this work, the boys were offered money for correct solutions.

Sometimes the caste the boy came from was announced, other times it was not. When the caste of the boys was publicly announced before the task took place, compared to not announced, there was a significant difference in performance. The number of mazes solved by lower-caste boys dropped by 25 per cent. In a further experiment, Hoff and Pandey introduced opportunities for risk-taking and challenge. In this situation, when caste was made salient, more lower-caste participants refused to gamble. So the social categories we are put into can not only affect our performance – as in the maze experiment – but also our expectations of positive outcomes – as in the gambling experiment.

What is dramatic here is that sociocultural labels made public can strongly influence our internal scripts for who we are and what we can do. Treating people as inferior surreptitiously creates in them a diminution of their self-worth, and this can diminish their self-efficacy, and sense of identity. Of course, this can apply to any social system, including systems of aid, which hierarchically categorize people according to arbitrary criteria or sets. Even though discrimination on the basis of caste is outlawed, Hoff and Pandey conclude by suggesting that common knowledge of the caste system remains, and holds back lower castes long after the original caste laws are abolished. Dominance is not only in the eyes of the beholder, but also of the beheld.

This process is part of a broader concept, 'stereotype threat'. The effect perhaps is familiar to many: whenever we sense that a person or group has us pigeonholed as inferior, that is stereotype threat. The very knowledge that we are objects to another – and inferior ones at that – can actually undermine our performance to such an extent that we end up confirming their stereotype. Bad teachers deriding their own pupils can achieve this, for example, if they keep it up for long enough, and so can aid workers (MacLachlan 1993a). In reality, of course, the person or group is often perfectly competent. When Hoff and Pandey's participants were not reminded about caste, they performed well. Capability, therefore, may be sustained, but social context partly determines performance. A context can be either enabling or hindering through its effects on sense of identity.

Reactance

In Figure 5.1, the term 'reactance' means that people do the opposite of what a constraining system tells them, or expects them, to do, as a way of reasserting their own freedom. Reactance is a way out of the first vicious circle in the model – exclusion–inclusion. By rebelling and doing the opposite of what we are 'supposed' to do, we reassert our choices. Sometimes this can include casting any so-called negative features in a positive light. Examples would be the revival of Scottish tartan, and the African-American movement 'Black is beautiful' during the 1970s. Each of these was arguably an attempt to take a so-called negative feature of identity and turn it into a positive feature – to celebrate it. What is celebrated is by definition positive, and can thereby elevate or lift one's sense of self and self-efficacy.

Leadership plays a key role in fostering reactance. Basu (2007), for example, suggests that a combination of affirmative action and positive role models can initiate and facilitate challenges to social dominance. We quoted one such positive role model at the start of this chapter, the Aboriginal leader Pat Dodson. Perhaps nowhere more than among the indigenous peoples of 'terra nullis' are the effects of an undermined identity more apparent. The chronic drug and alcohol abuse of many Aboriginals may be seen as symptomatic of being acculturated into a broader society that not only challenges but systematically undermines the value of your group, and therefore yourself, through assimilation and/or segregation (MacLachlan 2006). Against that drift is Pat Dodson's opening statement, 'We want health, housing, and education.' This is an assertion which challenges the stereotype of any 'handout mentality' among indigenous peoples – even to the extent of rejecting aid that threatens their culture. Instead, and as a foundation for enablement, Dodson implies that Aboriginal people want restorative social justice and are loud and proud in that claim.

Leadership may be helpful and even vital for social change to occur. Reactance does not necessarily depend, however, on recognized leaders – on either side – to find its expression. In our research on international aid, for example, we found that repeated exposure to aid may in itself be sufficient to cultivate reactance, and to do so quite directly, at a grassroots level (Carr et al. 1995). One person's gift is another's poison. Such findings are evidently important to examine more closely, because they might further illuminate how, and more importantly perhaps *why*, aid provokes the reactance it sometimes does.

During one of Malawi's famine-inducing droughts, anecdotes began to circulate about how some communities responded in an apparently contrary way to relief aid that was intended to 'help them to help themselves' (Kellogg Foundation 1992). The anecdotes included a town group which refused to unload its own aid consignment of food relief unless wages were paid for doing so; a village group which asked for payment to assemble some well equipment provided by an international development agency; academics who would attend development workshops only if they were paid a healthy per diem; and even children who asked for recompense for completing a school survey that had been designed, by an aid agency research team, to help improve educational services in their own school setting. From the point of view of reactance, these reactions could be described as heading in the opposite direction to those intended by the donor maxim, 'helping others to help themselves'. The revised script, it seemed, might be more like 'Pay us to help ourselves!' They might also, in part, be a way of changing stereotypical 'donor dependency' into something more positive, 'Pay me what I am worth!'

Whatever the precise interpretation we give them, anecdotes like these clearly imply that the understandings about aid held by donors and local communities were not completely aligned with each other (MacLachlan and Carr 2005). To test whether that might indeed be so, however, we put the anecdotes into a number of 'situational judgements'. We asked people from the local communities concerned in the stories themselves which reaction would be more likely. Would it be 'help us to help ourselves', a traditional watchword cum credo for international aid, or would it be 'pay me!', as our rumours and anecdotes had suggested?

The answers people gave were quite intriguing. Around one-fifth of all predictions, overall, were Pay Me. This is not a huge percentage. When we broke the percentages down by each scenario, however, one at a time, a different picture emerged. The lowest Pay Me reaction was in the rural, village well, scenario (11 per cent). Next came the school scenario, with 14 per cent – a slight increase. Then came the town scenario, unloading the food consignment, at 27 per cent. Last of all, with the highest predicted rate of Pay Me, came the academic conference scenario, at a 32 per cent prediction rate. When we tested this apparently climbing rate of Pay Me, there was in fact a statistically significant association between, on the one hand, exposure levels to aid agencies themselves (lowest for rural, highest for professional academics), and on the other the extent to which Pay Me reactions were being predicted by local people. In other words, at least in some cases, Pay Me may have been a reaction to, and form of reactance against, aid itself.

In a sense, such reactance could be seen as another aspect of double demotivation, and an attempt to restore justice to disparities in remuneration (see Chapter 4). Indeed, when we asked respondents why they made the judgements they did, their answers included that Pay Me could help reduce poverty. Also, however, Pay Me was seen as a way of giving a meaningful goal to work towards (remuneration, since much aid appeared to be pointless from a local perspective). This included motivating free riders in the group. Importantly too, Pay Me was seen as a reaction against the influence of Western economic values (a form of 'playing them at their own game'). Such responses, to us, seemed to be a way of restoring some pride and self-respect and autonomy in 'who we are and what we can do'. Not unlike Dodson's reactions, then, instead of 'gratitude' for aid that is designed to 'help people to help themselves', Pay Me may be a form of assertion that it is the *donor* who should be grateful – and perhaps respectful enough – to pay for the recipients' labour and time. Pay Me is reasserting identity (and making a buck!).

A downside to Pay Me, and other forms of reactance to injustice and social dominance, is that the person, group or institution is still, ultimately, dancing to some kind of majority tune. They continue to define themselves as the inverse of what they are 'supposed' to be – a kind of counter-stereotype, or anti-conformity. As African-American and 'black consciousness' writers like Fanon and Malcolm X have observed, these reactions are ultimately not completely freely chosen. In a sense, however fair and justified they may be, they are not, yet, representations of real 'freedom as development' in its fullest possible sense.

Conversion

To complete the process of liberation from defining ourselves as 'not-other' may require more leadership. Leadership does play a role in much social change and social justice. Challenges like Dodson's, according to Figure 5.1, must be consistent. Provided they persist for long enough, hard enough and coherently enough, the powerful group, institution or individual will eventually find themselves questioning their own, implicit assumptions, their own myths (see Chapter 3). This is a form of mental unfreezing, as people in the majority begin to question their own assumptions, past actions and inactions. One of the key stumbling blocks in Aboriginal–Balanda ('White fella') relationships in Australia has been a refusal on the part of the Australian government to apologize for the human rights abuses perpetrated in the past. Recently, however, the government did make an apology. Some real political leadership was displayed, and injustice was at least overtly recognized, justice respected. Although the apology should, of course, have come much earlier, leadership and justice restoration are mutual processes. Leaders, on both sides, will now hopefully continue to play a role in healing these particular soul wounds.

There is a risk in leadership here, of course, that it will be all talk and no action. When the apology was made, there were, and are, detractors. Such resistance, a reversion or regression to social dominance, will probably continue. There is a more insidious form of resistance, however. Even within the best-intended institutions, groups and individuals, actions do not always match words. An everyday example from work groups is when the rhetoric of team-work (in company plans, departmental away days, recruitment and selection, etc.) is not really matched by actual practices (which remain as hierarchical as they were before). The result, in workplaces at least, is often demotivation and cynicism (Boggs et al. 2005).

The same might apply in aid projects and workplaces. An example is described by Eyben and León (2005). They recount their experiences of working on a UK-funded project to promote democracy in the national elections in Bolivia in 2002. The donors sought to establish a project that would promote the participation of marginalized groups, by encouraging them to vote. Perhaps there was concern that those who might be encouraged to vote were less likely to vote for the government party in power, than they were for opposition parties. Of course, there is never just one source of conflict; rather differences and division are conflated and work themselves into intermingled disputes that reflect a number of different agendas. Another interpretation of the difficulty that arose from the proposed project, however, is that the national government undermined this project because they did not feel sufficient ownership of it. Ownership of course implies entitlement, and to that extent, from Figure 5.1, has implications for justice:

> While giving, the owner was also keeping. That process of giving both expressed and transformed patterns of personal and organizational relationships. The gift itself has a bright and shadow side, expressed in terms of solidarity, trust, and affection on the one hand, and betrayal, anger and aggression on the other. Yet, if you were to read the official donor agency records concerning this project, we would find a logical framework, indicators of achievement and 'neutral' evaluations. A peculiar sanitation would have occurred that presents a plausible fiction of a rational bureaucracy making informed value for money judgements as to the most effective and efficient means of achieving poverty-reducing outcomes. (2005: 14–15)

Gaps between rhetoric and reality can be found elsewhere in aid. The nomenclature of 'development cooperation' and 'partnership' may try to eschew the idea of givers and receivers, donors and recipients, in the name of Basu's participative equity. Some prefer to construct aid as an investment that will have longer-term returns for the investor. Yet the human dynamics of these transactions continue to resonate in the force field between gifts and entitlements.

Eyben and León (2005) suggest that this change in language is 'symptomatic of the essential discomfort that those involved feel about the anomaly of a gift relationship' (p. 111). Our point is that honesty and courage are needed to address such unmentionables, not only from leaders but also from the proverbial troops on both sides. Speaking the unspoken involves a bit of 'terror management' for everyone. Pay Me, of course, may be a way of 'speaking a truth to power'; against aid-preserving dominance, encroaching on justice and undermining social identity. Such issues need to be acknowledged, though, by those in power, i.e. donors, who may need to relax their grip and hand over more power to the local community. The reflective lesson in Pay Me reactions, and thus in Figure 5.1, is that there has to be genuine – not merely rhetorical – reciprocity in all forms of exchange. Thus Reactance and Conversion (converting to a different view), our mid-level interlocking dynamic of circles illustrated in Figure 5.1, begin to position the drive for *justice* firmly in the domain of *identity*.

Capacity and capability

In Figure 5.1, one way in which aid can work is by helping to build 'capacity' (Manning 2006). In recent years, the ethos of 'technical assistance' has been replaced by attempts to build the capacity of local people – rather than foreigners – to address their own problems: 'Capacity building is about enabling people to rediscover their strengths and limitations, and empowering them to take control of their lives and develop their fullest potential' (Angeles 2005: 52). This definition is perhaps too individualistic. The United Nations Development Programme (UNDP 1997: 3) offers a more inclusive definition: 'the process by which individuals, organizations, institutions and societies develop abilities (individually and collectively) to perform functions, solve problems and set and achieve objectives'. This definition more explicitly embraces social systems and institutions. While some prefer 'capacity development' to 'capacity building', because they feel the latter implies a lack of existing capacity (clearly a patronizing stance), we do not agree. Capacity can always be built, and building does not imply greenfield sites.

In our view (see Chapter 1) capacity development is inherently mutual. An example of this reciprocity in capacity building can be found in the work of the Office of Aboriginal Development, in Far North Australia (Ivory 2003). Ivory's job was to visit remote indigenous communities in the Australian outback, and to facilitate enterprise development in those settings. At first glance, and perhaps with one or two stereotypes in tow, such a task might be an uphill struggle. Yet in practice the project turned out quite the reverse, with many enterprises getting off the ground. Some of this success can be put down to the approach adopted in the project itself. The ethos of the project was genuinely participatory (no social dominance) and respectful (of local values and culture – justice). No attempt was made to 'train' people in what to do in order to start a business. Emphasis was instead put on how to negotiate government red tape in order to get a business started. The unspoken assumption is that Aboriginal people already have the capability to develop an enterprise; all that is required is a facilitating environment – not red tape – to let it out. By using flip charts on how to navigate the bureaucratic maze in Canberra, competencies were more easily turned into enterprising performance.

Much of the foundation for the enterprises' development was in pre-existing cultural identity. Ivory knew that for centuries before so-called '*terra nullius*', the indigenous peoples of Far North Australia had thriving trade routes up into southern and south-eastern Asia. Enterprise values were, and still are, deeply embedded in cultural identity. From that humble point of view, aligned in knowledge, and respectful in practice, Ivory's approach made perfect sense. And it paid off. Many enterprises were enabled, ranging from indigenous cosmetics to eco-tourism (for details, see ibid.). These enterprises were not run along Balanda lines. Their goals were in keeping with social achievement, insofar as profits went back into the local community, and the company enabled the development of community pride. In that sense, perhaps, the developments in Far North Australia are quite resonant of, and indeed consistent with, the African concept of *uMunthu* (Mji et al. 2009).

From an identity perspective, the businesses that developed reflected a healthy combination of traditional values that were 'fit for purpose' in a global economy – for example, cosmetics and tourism. They were neither assimilated into 'mainstream' businesses, nor isolated from modern markets. They were a blend of global and local, freely chosen by the local people, and in that sense far from reactance. In theories of social change, including theories of socio-economic development, such changes are regarded as 'integrated', because they manage to integrate the old with the new, the local with the global, a 'glocality' (Carr 2004). In business, such mergers are called a 'win-win' outcome. Such outcomes, as the names suggest, build capacity and capability on both sides: the indigenous community benefits as well as the wider community, both in Australia (e.g. via increased export earnings, enhanced social reputation) and beyond (e.g. international tourists are able to appreciate more of indigenous culture and customs, stereotypes are reduced, etc.). Hence, through a process of reciprocal exchange, majority as well as minority groups 'developed', their capabilities (or posibilities) increased.

Case example

In his recent book *The Life You Can Save: Acting now to end world poverty*, the philosopher and social activist Peter Singer describes an occupation termed 'rag-picker' in the strengthening economy of India (2008). Rag-pickers scrape a subsistence-level existence picking scraps of rubbish from local refuse tips, and selling them wherever they can in order to survive. These workers are often from the lowest caste in India, the Dalits, and they have frequently been treated with 'contempt … exploited economically, and sexually harassed by the dealers to whom they sold their gleanings' (ibid.: 95). A project funded by Oxfam Australia was therefore set up in order to try to reverse some of these indignities in poverty.

The project focused on the organization and mobilization of labour. The original goal had been to provide literacy classes, but Oxfam realized that more basic needs might be addressed instead. The first task was to help the women organize themselves into a Registered Association of Rag-pickers. This enabled some group protection and a rise in the prices that they were able to secure. They were paid 1 rupee, or 3 US cents, for a kilogram of plastic. Some of this money was invested in clean clothes, which Singer reports contrasted vividly with the squalor of the rubbish tips that formed their workplace. The registration of an association also enabled the group to approach the local municipal council, and to secure the right to carry identity cards. These enabled them to gain entry to apartment buildings, in which they were able to expand their job activities to include household recycling. This meant a cleaner and healthier workplace, collecting recyclable material directly from people's homes instead of an unsanitary and risk-laden rubbish tip. With this improved access to product and market, income improved. The association was also able to expand its activities further, including setting up a savings scheme for the workers and access to micro-credit. The interest from the savings was used to support school attendance (scholarships) and books for the members' children. Before the project, these children had worked alongside their mothers at the city dump.

When Singer met with the rag-pickers, they informed him that they had decided that the involvement of Oxfam was at an end. Although they deeply appreciated the support that Oxfam had given, the original goals had now been attained because the Registered Association of Rag-pickers had become '*self*-supporting' (ibid.: 95, emphasis added).

Case analysis

In terms of Figure 5.1, unprotected, unorganized rag-pickers, prior to the project, inhabited the margins of local society and economy. They literally picked a living from the refuse of others, and were exploited and abused by a range of shadowy figures. Their attempts to earn a living in a money economy were not respected. Their attempts at inclusion were rebutted, by relatively powerful vested interests whose interests were best served by maintaining exclusion. In Figure 5.1, these are the top two circles, the dynamics of Dominance.

The arrival of the Oxfam project, led by Laxmi Narayan, a lecturer in adult education at a nearby university, changed the situation. She came originally with the idea of providing classes in literacy, a medium- to longer-term solution to getting out of poverty. This kind of intervention was deemed less pressing than enabling the women to self-organize into a labour collective. From that moment on, the women reportedly took pride in their appearance, even while working on the rubbish dumps. They were furthermore able to negotiate a pay rise for how much they earned for each kilogram of plastic picked. In terms of Figure 5.1, this can be understood as reactance against the stereotype of rag-pickers, and the aid agency and project, headed by Laxmi, was open minded enough to change its idea of what was needed, to make it more aligned with local needs and aspiration. Not unlike the women in other forms of work collective (V. Schein 2003), the women found refuge precisely in their so-called 'weak point' – being women. In terms of Figure 5.1, these forms of repositioning, in reactance to continued oppression and social dominance, are the dynamics of Justice.

As well as marking forms of justice, the changes above also reflect the development – or rather, redevelopment – of identity. A symbolic but also palpable indicator of these developments in identity is the arrival of an identity card. This card was won as a result of negotiating and bargaining with the local council. In one sense, its acquisition represents a form of conversion on the part of the local council, in recognizing the identity and dignity of the rag-pickers' occupation. Aided in part by actions from managers in Oxfam, their campaign for decent work had enabled them to secure a right to enter apartments where they could access raw materials for their products directly, and of course more safely. This change then began to spiral in a positive sense that enabled the development of their own capacities, and those of their children: they secured enough capital to pump-prime a range of further initiatives, such as sending their kids to school to obtain a decent education. As has been argued by Sen (1999), changes like this will in time improve local capacity and capabilities (Figure 5.1).

Perhaps the ultimate litmus test of the capacity-building project was the fact that the group itself asked for the project aid to be withdrawn. They had the autonomy and sense of identity to say please take the aid to another, more needy group. There was no Pay Me, no rejection of the aid. Far from it – the aid was accepted precisely because it had *not* been too intrusive, dominant, unjust or demeaning. In the process, Oxfam too was changed, first from potentially pushing a project that might have been too large a leap at the time (full-scale literacy for the rag-picker occupational group) to a more 'incremental improvement', inherently more aligned with more pressing local needs (see Chapter 7). Second, the organization had not only helped capacity to develop itself in the local setting, it had also, in all probability, developed its *own* capacity to manage future projects of this nature, and to help to promote the development of dignity for organized labour. Organizational learning like this is discussed in detail in the next chapter. For the present, our main point is that capacity building recognized existing capabilities and added to them.

Figure 5.1, with its three pairs of circles interacting in a hierarchical fashion, presents a way of thinking through the dynamics not just of dominance, justice and identity, but also of some of the factors that involved these dynamics – the 'causes of the causes'. Our aim here is not to claim that these factors are always implicated in the causes of 'development' projects as we have described above; rather, our aim has been to illustrate how systems thinking, even in necessarily complex and perhaps even chaotic social circumstances, can provide insights into the human dynamics that can facilitate and empower human development.

Of course, analysing a case is one thing, pulling out helpful learning from it is another. One thing we have learnt from the above example of rag-pickers is the importance of advocacy skills. In effect, both Ivory (2003) and Narayan (above) had focused on helping people to navigate the system, to get their voice into the decision-making process. Such skills are arguably heavily in demand in impoverished workplace settings. The International Labour Organization (ILO), for instance, recently adopted as its 2009 annual conference theme 'Decent Work'. Decent work is promoted, for example, by enabling the skills to negotiate and bargain, and generally argue for one's point of view – one's identity – to be respected (Yiu and Saner 2005).

We hope that this book's end-users will include the ILO's 'constituents': ministries of labour, employers' associations, trade unions, civil society groups, and of course workers' groups like the indigenous people of the Northern Territory in Australia, and the rag-pickers in India. As Yiu and Saner point out, fostering decent work, including decent pay and working conditions, is an integral component of the Millennium Development Goals in particular, and poverty reduction in general. Key skills that can be facilitated include, for example, persuasive communication, negotiating and bargaining, conflict resolution, political skills, like networking, and group decision-making. Their manual is an outstanding example of how and where useful interventions can sensitively be made; by helping others to *identify* themselves.

The roles and processes of identification just described are not restricted, of course, to rights at and to work. Advocacy skills are also in demand in other 'life spaces'. In the context of broader social inclusion and identity, we have also stressed the importance of disabled people's organizations in Bolivia, among the most marginalized groups in that country, working together through reciprocal empowerment and advocacy activities (Griffiths et al. 2009) to attain improvements in health, education, transport and so on. Another of the projects we are involved with – APODD: African Policy on Disability and Development (www.a-podd.org) – explicitly seeks to pinpoint empowerment and influence pathways for putting disability on the 'development agenda'. Identity, advocacy and social inclusion are keystones for the social development and human rights of many marginalized groups. We believe that one of the keys to the success of Poverty Reduction Strategy Papers (PRSPs) will be the effective promoting of marginalized groups' sense of identity, ownership and empowerment. Such community voice, and activism, has long featured centrally in development initiatives across Latin America (Sánchez et al. 2003), influenced by the liberation pedagogy of Paulo Freire (1972).

Returning to the second of our opening quotes in this chapter, aid workers are bearers of cultural contact as well as the aid they bring. In fact, the aid itself is imbued with cultural values and assumptions. This means that there is room for cross-cultural training in order to minimize the potential for harm. Typically, cultural competence is seen as having at least three main components: (1) awareness, (2) knowledge and (3) skill. We see this in our opening quotation, '*He doesn't know it*, but he's not alone' (MacLachlan 2002, emphasis added). Cultural training can also be effective in reducing stereotyping, witting or not. Reflecting social dominance perhaps, the training is usually reserved for the foreigner, not the local host, who is also the economically poorer 'partner'. It can be argued that awareness training, like all forms of cross-cultural preparation, should morally and practically be provided for *both* parties in any cross-cultural exchange (Selmer, forthcoming). After all, both expatriate *and* local people have to deal with cross-cultural diversity. Inequalities in training opportunity and access to the training would not only help to perpetuate dominance, but would also impinge on equity and justice. Such dynamics can 'multiply up' to organizational, community and institutional levels. Hence groups (such as communities and organizations) and institutions (such as major development agencies, or professions like aid worker or social worker) can be culturally competent, or incompetent, too. As we saw in the second of our opening quotes, theories of development and human development, achievement, etc., can be saturated with cultural assumptions that may not sit well within local cultural models, and especially the identities therein.

Turning specifically to justice, we have seen that there is a reasonable likelihood that social dominance will facilitate cultural reactance. Sometimes, such reactance is well adapted and perfectly appropriate. For example, we have seen how the rag-pickers deliberately reacted against stereotypes that they themselves would be dressed in rags. In another instance, research on immigrants from lower- to higher-income economies has found that when the host community is entrenched in its expectations that migrants will remain on the periphery, even when they first 'try on' some aspects of the host culture, then remaining apart and simply reasserting their own identity can be good for mental health (Berry, forthcoming).

Figure 5.1 implies that reasserting one's identity may be a necessary trigger for changing the frame of mind among relatively powerful, socially dominant groups. Nevertheless, there will be occasions when reactance remains just that – anti-conformity, which is still partly determined by the outside agency, the socially dominant group. The 'unmentionable' or potentially uncomfortable truth being implied in Figure 5.1 is that some forms of cultural reassertion may be overstated and, in effect, determined by an agenda that is ultimately outside, not inside, indigenous identity itself (Tajfel 1978). The concept of reactance in Figure 5.1 suggests that for identity to be reasserted in the fullest sense there must be a progression beyond reactance, beyond defining the group as simply not-X (where X is the majority out-group). Which elements of cultural identity are central and distinctive must be chosen and emphasized freely and independently (Fanon 1965).

Resisting oppression and injustice, by whatever means, has to produce a reaction in the majority. Lip-service on their part, to participative social equity, will not be sufficient for actual behaviour to change. What Figure 5.1 implies is that it will be easier to simply 'say' that development practice is equalitarian, participative, equitable, aligned, etc., etc. Development policy will be at risk of not being translated into practice. Such rhetoric without substance is a powerful demotivator – for example, cynicism and disengagement by local people identifying with local cultures and turning away from 'development' institutions. Translating policy into development practice will require, in effect, a process of disempowerment of the dominant. A key element in this process, and one which we have not given sufficient attention to thus far, is civil society, or NGOs – non-governmental organizations. NGOs are particularly relevant to the idea of identity, because not only do they offer an alternative identity in aid, but also one that is often claimed to be more grounded and closer to individuals and communities. As we will see, however, the identity politics of civil society is also a factor in international aid and development.

Identity and civil society

Local identities are often lost in the cauldron of democratization through national parliaments and legislatures, which decide how to represent and describe 'all the people' rather than particular groups, with particular needs and identities. Sometimes, of course, there is no governmental pretence of equal representation, and at other times governments actively oppress, rape, murder and exercise genocide against their own citizenry. The idea of relatively small organizations representing the needs of marginalized groups, especially of those with little or no 'voice', is particularly attractive; it is tied to intrinsic aspects of their identity and the achievement of human rights. Such 'identities', or values, can stretch much farther than this, to include, for instance, the mechanisms of aid (e.g. a community school in one country helping a community school in another), or reasons for giving aid (to develop business capacity or because of religious conviction). These non-governmental initiatives often reflect and seek to promote what is good in society, and in so doing to create a more *civil* society, one that is more inclusive, progressive, caring.

Contrast this description of civil society with the idea, often heard but rarely spoken, that 'NGOs are more a part of the problem than part of the solution' to the challenge of development. We are now going to consider what this means, how we got here and what all this has got to do with identity – and whose identity?

Lewis (2005) notes that the lack of clarity regarding just what an NGO 'is' constitutes a major problem: 'non-profit', 'voluntary', 'third sector', 'civil society', 'faith-based organizations', 'community-based organizations', 'development agencies' are terms that can all overlap and morph to support or challenge arguments, especially those concerned with effectiveness and resource allocation. The NGO label can also be applied to philanthropic organizations, churches, hospitals, schools and quasi-government organizations (or 'quangos').

Eric Werker and Faisal Ahmed (2008) see NGOs as private organizations that act pro-socially in 'developing countries', and as the subset of the broader non-profit sector working in international development. They distinguish NGOs from community-based organizations, because, unlike NGOs, the latter seek to directly benefit their members. Thus, according to Werker and Ahmed, NGOs are a subgroup of civil society. As this definition suits our purposes in this book, that is the one we shall work with. While conceptual focusing is important, however, even then we are left with a huge range of organizational types and scale. For instance, some 'indigenous' (generally meaning 'non-Western/Northern') NGOs are staffed by one or two people, there are five US-based NGOs whose expenditures in 2004 exceeded $500 million: Feed the Children, World Vision, Food for the Poor, Catholic Relief Services and CARE, in descending order of expenditure (ibid.).

Bertin Martens addressed the simple, but incredibly complex (!), question 'Why do aid agencies exist?'. His answer is that, primarily, they mediate the 'diverging preferences between donors and recipients'. This clearly resonates with the case study of the DfID-funded aid project in Bolivia, described above, and details – diverging preferences of the gift 'givers' and gift 'receivers' – recall our earlier discussion of 'who owns the gift'. In a sense, therefore, NGOs are the 'middlemen' of the aid industry, having to skilfully negotiate with sometimes diverging agendas, but doing so in a way that acknowledges the values and identity of the donors (otherwise NGOs would be out of income) and the values and identity of recipients (otherwise NGOs would be out of 'outputs' – they would have nowhere to do their business).

Aid is big business. Easterly and Tobias (2008) report that foreign aid from official sources (that is, excluding private aid) amounted to $103.6 billion in 2006. They calculate that, over the past fifty years, measured in 2006 dollars, over $2.3 million has been spent in official aid. In 2006, $87.7 billion was given by governments, worldwide, as official aid. In the United States, which gave $19.7 billion of this, 15 per cent was channelled through NGOs, with a further 18 per cent going through intergovernmental organizations (e.g. the World Bank or the United Nations) (Werker and Ahmed 2008).

Werker and Ahmed (ibid.) note that NGOs, working in the 'development' context, are often idealized as organizations that are willing to set aside profits or politics for the sake of 'doing good'. They may be seen as 'magic bullets' (Edwards and Hulme 1996: 3) for a failing development process, and as being more efficient at providing goods and services than governmental alternatives. Werker and Ahmed, however, suggest that 'This romantic view is too starry-eyed' (2008: 74). They report OECD figures that show that the level of discretionary funding that rich countries have given NGOs working in 'development' have risen from negligible levels in the 1950s to over $2 billion now. Broader civil society has also achieved much greater political influence, with civil society involvement in World Bank projects rising from just 6 per cent in the late 1980s to 70 per cent in 2006 (ibid.). Aid from governments dwarfs that from philanthropy, with the international – outside the United States – spend of the three largest-spending foundations, Gates, Ford and Kellogg, reaching just $188 million, $162 million and

$45 million, respectively, in 2005 (ibid., citing Foundation Centre, 2006). But the funding model of NGOs also differs considerably, with, for instance, some benefiting from very large donations from particular organizations, governments or individuals, while Food for the Poor, which has a funding base of around three million people, gains much more modest support.

Werker and Ahmed (ibid.) contrast the work functions, identified from surveys conducted on samples, of the 3,159 NGOs registered in Uganda with those of the 6,590 registered in Bangladesh. While 'raising awareness' was, for instance, an activity reported by a similar 97 and 92 per cent of NGOs in Uganda and Bangladesh respectively, there were significant differences with regard to other activities. The respective reporting of 'advocacy and lobbying' (60 per cent versus 31 per cent), 'credit and financing' (33 per cent versus 92 per cent), 'water and sanitation' (11 per cent versus 51 per cent), healthcare (16 per cent versus 55 per cent) and 'employment facilitation' (8 per cent versus 47 per cent) testifies to significant differences in how NGOs operate in different countries. While it can be challenging to measure the value of NGOs' distinctive activities in terms of things like water and sanitation, it becomes much more difficult to measure the effects of activities such as raising awareness or advocacy. So, the idea of NGOs as go-betweens that necessarily represent the situation, feelings and aspirations of marginalized groups is not likely to be true in all cases. NGOs, like everyone else, have agendas, and these agendas arise, at least in part, from those aspects of their identity that they see as crucial. An obvious example would be that Catholic agencies are inclined not to supply condoms or support abortion services in low-income countries – it goes against their Catholic identity and against the sort of identity that the agency would like the recipients of its aid to have.

In an increasingly overpopulated field, NGOs are constantly striving to assert a distinctive identity. Some NGOs, for example, pride themselves on reaching the most remote areas and providing services to the poorest and most disadvantaged. This is a laudable goal, but attempting to overcome the obstacles to achieving it can cause problems. If we take an NGO attempting to deliver com-prehensive healthcare in a remote mountainous region of Lesotho, for example, there is no infrastructure, poor communication and transport, all leading to difficulty recruiting and retaining staff, so they decide to offer higher salaries to attract health workers. The unintended impact of this is that the surrounding communities are denuded of health worker staff as they scramble to take up the new, higher-paid positions. This is a common problem with health NGOs operating in an environment where human resources are scarce. In Lesotho, 44 per cent of respondents said they have seriously thought about leaving the hospital or clinic where they are currently working, and more than half of the respondents said they are actively seeking other employment. In Malawi, almost a quarter of the sample said they are very likely to leave their job within the next year (McAuliffe et al. 2009b). A common sentiment is expressed by a clinical officer:

> Once I finish my internship I will leave the public service [for] the NGO. My colleagues in the NGO earn MWK [kwacha] 80,000 a month, while I earn MWK 21,000 a month. Though I have better chances to further my education in the public sector, I can still do the same working with the NGO by saving more than half of my salary for two years. My colleague did the same and is back in the university while his mates in the public sector are still waiting for their turn to be trained from the [Ministry of Health].

The Advisory Group on Civil Society and Aid Effectiveness (2008) suggests that there are over one million CSOs (civil society organizations) in India and 200,000 in the Philippines. The idea of these having a shared, harmonized 'identity' is certainly problematic. From our perspective, what is important is that the identity of NGOs is clear and that the implications of this identity for interventions are made more explicit. Only then can we establish harmonization between donors, and alignment between the needs and cultural values of recipients and civil society organizations.

The International Civil Society Steering Group for the Accra High Level Forum (2008) called for all aid to be united, its predictability enhanced, and greater attention paid to the 'cross-cutting' issues of human rights, social inclusion and gender equality. The report also critically highlights aid conditionalities as a barrier to country ownership, the need for increased transparency to promote mutual accountability and a meaningful policy dialogue, and for a rebalancing of the power relationships between donors and partner countries. It also highlights the need for independent assessment of commitments made to the Paris Declaration on Aid Effectiveness. The Advisory Group on Civil Society and Aid Effectiveness (2008: i–ii) suggests that:

> The underlying development model of the Paris Declaration is one in which donors and governments work together closely to implement national development plans under national government leadership. … it flags CSOs as potential participants in the identification of priorities and the monitoring of development programmes. However, it does not recognize CSOs as development actors in their own right, with their own priorities, programmes and partnership arrangements.

They go on to say that the Paris Declaration '… fails to take into account the rich diversity of social interveners in a democratic society and fails to recognize the full range of roles played by CSOs as development actors and change agents' (ibid.: ii). The group claim that 'CSOs are often particularly effective at reaching the poor and socially excluded, mobilizing community efforts, speaking up for human rights and gender equality, and helping to empower particular constituencies' (ibid.: ii). If this is true then civil society has a critical role to play in empowering marginalized groups, in supporting and perhaps developing their cultural identity, for culture should not be some unchanging historical artefact (MacLachlan 2006). Our point here is that, equally, the identity of civil society needs to be integrated and supported, where it fits well with the aspirations of the communities it seeks to work with. As will be seen in Chapter 6, this is not always the case.

It is often difficult to speak poorly of the good, and so few have sought to critically reflect on the possible negative consequences of NGO activities. Mendelson and Glenn (2002) argue that foreign-funded NGOs (focusing on democracy-building in eastern Europe) have created domestic offshoots that are well funded but which, ironically, have little grassroots support. Rocha Menochal and Rogerson (2006) draw attention to the fact that in the opinion of

Southern or indigenous CSOs, international NGOs are increasingly perceived as competing with local CSOs for resources, and in doing so are undermining the growth and effectiveness of an independent and autonomous indigenous civil society sector. Gauri and Galef (2005) have suggested that micro-finance managers in Bangladesh are incentivized to make loans to wealthier clients, rather than the poorest of the poor. Barber and Bowie (2008), in a critical commentary on international NGOs, suggest that 'the impetus for the activities of these NGOs is not really the situation in Malawi or Mali (similar situations could be found in 50 other countries), but the demands of their donors. In order to stay in business donors must be satisfied' (p. 749). They argue that the absence of regulatory frameworks or the difficulty of enforcing them where they exist means that they cannot change the behaviour of these NGOs, and even if they were to try 'they are often dissuaded by the embassy of the donor country' (ibid.: 749).

Werker and Ahmed (2008) write: 'Most publicly available programme evaluations by NGOs ... are descriptive, rarely contain rigorous statistical analysis, and almost never report strong negative outcomes. A more scientific and transparent approach to these studies might present a clearer appraisal of NGO programmes' (p. 87). They continue: 'the paucity of clear, objective evaluations should not be particularly surprising. It is in neither the interests of NGOs, nor the official donor agency (complicit as a funder), to publicize less-than-stellar results' (p. 87).

Perhaps there is little demand for rigorous evaluation of NGO activities because, generally, the public view, both in rich and poorer countries, is overwhelmingly benevolent. Sometimes, perhaps not that often, this view is not justified. But a more critical consideration of how NGOs see themselves, and how the public in general should see them – in other words a more considered view of their identity and functioning – might help to contribute towards achieving their goals.

Werker and Ahmed (ibid.) put this more forcefully: 'Nongovernmental organizations seem to represent the best of private citizens responding to global inequities. But behind the characteristics inherent to an NGO model of development are lurking several challenges: too many actors, too many chiefs and too much mission.' The 'too many actors' refers to the massive number of NGOs that we have already noted, a number that has grown, and continues to grow, at a steady rate. 'Too many chiefs' refers to the number of agency agendas and the numerous ways in which they can work with each other. We have previously discussed the idea of the 'aid chain' (Carr et al. 1998), which can comprise either a linear sequence or a more complex matrix of interlocking agencies. So the simpler linear sequence might be taxpayer (you) – bilateral agency (e.g. Irish Aid) – intergovernmental organization (e.g. the WHO) – international NGO (e.g. Concern) – local NGO – goods and services to poor and/or disadvantaged people. 'How many dollars from the initial transfer actually reach the final beneficiary is anybody's guess' (ibid.: 88). 'Too much mission' refers to the idea that NGOs know what is best for their intended beneficiaries, but that different NGOs know different things, and that these things are often more driven by ideology than by needs assessments where poor people participate in identifying those needs. Agency agendas can be 'colonialistic' in the sense that they are trying to get others to think as they do. This is not because they are 'bad' but because most of us, particularly those who have made a huge commitment to working in aid, have an emotional as well as an intellectual commitment to it, and both of these are braided into the identity of the organizations we work for.

Perhaps the next stage in development of NGO activity will be along the lines described by Tom Arnold (2008), the CEO of Concern Worldwide. He notes that Concern started its operation in Biafra, where they offered technical assistance. Concern then moved into a phase of capacity building through partnership; they are now increasingly in a situation where they are a catalyst – bringing together other actors to make things happen – and an influencer of development policies. Concern works through and with others with a philosophy of '3 Is': Innovation, Influence and Impact. Through four programme areas health, education, livelihoods and HIV/ AIDS – Concern is currently reaching approximately 28 million people, many of whom are the poorest of the poor. This is a staggering achievement, particularly when the identity of the organization may in a sense be becoming more 'backgrounded' – they are the enablers, less than the doers, and may have to enable between organizations with very different identities and missions. In this tricky and demanding scenario the enablers of aid and development will have difficult choices to make ahead: 'The most important single indicator of improvement will be reductions in the number of agencies competing on the ground' (Moore 2007: 46). It will also be more difficult for them to evade issues of effectiveness and accountability.

Brand aid

In our discussion of organizational learning in the next chapter we will see how aid agencies, while sometimes cooperating, also sometimes compete against each other for resources, position and the donor attention of their government(s) and public(s). In Chapter 3, our consideration of dominance noted the role of celebrity recognition, as if a celebrity with the 'right' image could enhance the awareness of, and perhaps also, the image of an aid agency. In a competitive market the need to distinguish your activity results in branding. McDonald's and Starbucks are different, we are told, not just because they provide different products, but because the sorts of products they provide have different connotations. Aid agencies are also brands, sometimes incidentally, sometimes much more deliberately, but as with the driver of the Land Rover in one of the opening quotes to this chapter, or the cynical critique of Oxfam (Box 1.1), the identity that others ascribe to aid agencies can be very important (Carr and Rugimbana 2009). Trust, for example, can be a significant influence on donation behaviour and other forms of public support (Burt and Dunham 2009).

Levine (2009) is critical of the approach developed by the Bush administration, particularly the president's Emergency Plan for AIDS Relief and the Millennium Challenge Account, where she says 'branding has become rampant', and she calls instead for rebranding; in fact, she says the Obama administration should 'unbrand'. She explains: 'Unbranding means ending the practice of using multiple logos and labeling projects with clever acronyms ... It is honestly quite hard to believe aid programs are "country owned" or follow a coherent "whole of government" approach when every poster,

SUV, training manual and building sign is covered with a half-dozen seals of U.S. organizations.' This clearly also relates to our earlier discussion of 'who owns the gift' – the giver or the receiver? On the giver's side it is, however, important for them to be able to demonstrate to taxpayers or other donors just where their money is being spent. Thus, much humanitarian aid from USAID has 'Gift from the American people' printed on it.

On the receiving side, if buildings or equipment have foreign logos emblazoned across them, one could understand how it might be thought in the receiving country that this signifies ownership by someone else – say the donating agency – and so this might be taken to imply that the local community need not get involved in their maintenance or use. It might also, of course, undermine the country's government and any sense of their accountability to their own citizenry; as it may appear, it is not the government doing this – for better or for worse – but a foreign power. Levine (ibid.) suggests that to rebrand America, there is a need to 'make the stuff procured with our aid dollars look more like it belongs to the countries we're trying to help and less like pop-up ads for U.S.A. Inc. and its wholly-owned subsidiaries'.

Vestergaard (2008) argues that at the same time as the practice of for-profit organizations is becoming increasingly ethical, the practice of not-for-profit organizations is becoming increasingly commercialized. She sees humanitarian organizations torn between the need for visibility, with its greater dependence on the media, and the implications of 'compassion fatigue' for their donor publics. Aid agencies, in a highly competitive niche, need to be recognized, they need to have profile, maintain visibility; that is, they need a market-able identity. As we have seen in Chapter 3, celebrities are often used to bring to market the ideas that an aid agency is selling.

Aid brands need to generate trust and respect, as these are the attributes that will help secure donations (Anisya and Fritz 2006). Even once a strong brand image is established, however, it can still be very fragile. Anisya and Fritz suggested that in 2005 Oxfam GB declined a number of free aircraft trips to carry humanitarian cargo because it couldn't verify that the planes had not previously been used to transport arms. Similarly aid agencies may be wary of receiving donations from companies that might tarnish their own brand image, such as those involved in weapons or cigarette manufacturing.

Brand image in aid is not just about identity, it's also about dominance. In the transnational aid marketplace it's important for some types of aid to be seen as better, more effective or more authoritative, than other types. In the same way that regular designer brands thrive on the connotations of their brand – on what the purchase of that brand says about the purchaser – which aid agencies you choose to support (if any) may be read as a commentary on you. It is an uncomfortable thought, but a survival imperative, that some of the larger aid agencies need to 'keep down' some of the smaller aid agencies, so that they can survive in the marketplace of donor attention.

Ecker-Ehrhardt (2007) discusses how journalists articulate a 'humanitarian authority structure' which incorporates governmental institutions, UN agencies and humanitarian NGOs. The UN, however, is seen as having an institutional structure that makes its various agencies part of a universal whole – 'a "brand" of its own with a high recall value'. The consequence of this is that the symbolic authority of the UN seems more compelling, to both individual citizens and national leaders, compared to that of any individual NGO. The 'compelling' nature of aid agencies such as Unicef, the Red Cross and Oxfam effectively enables them to be 'designer aid brands'. The 'Change for Good' alliance between British Airways and Unicef shows how top-end brands from distinct markets can mutually benefit from such an association, and in so doing raise an admirable amount of money. Some might therefore consider the UN to be competing with much smaller NGOs, and in doing so to be effectively undermining their sustainability. Interestingly, according to Ecker-Ehrhardt, the oft-cited 'NGO-ization' of international aid is much less reflected in journalists' opinions than the UN.

Slim (2003) suggests that the conventional and critical skills of diplomacy and humanitarian argument practised by many aid agencies should be augmented by some of the principles of marketing and personal selling. Of particular relevance here, he sees the marketing challenge for brands like the Red Cross, the United Nations, Oxfam and Médecins Sans Frontières (which he identifies as among the strongest brands in the world) as being to make sure that the brand says what they want it to say. He explains that

> modern marketing sees the power and vitality of a brand as coming from the fact that the word brand is regarded … as a verb and not a noun. A company or a humanitarian agency needs to brand all it does and not simply to rely on having a brand … For example … everything the Red Cross does should be actively reaffirming this message whenever and wherever it comes into contact with anyone. (Ibid.: 12)

This imperative of assertive branding – as a verb – is problematic not just because of the dominance and identity issues noted above, but also because of the governance issues – the disjunction between citizens and those who 'provide for them'. Perhaps we can distinguish between aid branding at the points of demand and supply. Retaining brand competition – and sometimes quite healthy competition – in terms of contracting can be distinguished from the delivery of aid, where buildings, SUVs and technology can be 'supporting the people of …'; supporting their identity and bringing good governance and maintenance of resources to the fore.

Conclusion

We began this chapter with the idea that every gift takes something away. A behavioural cost–benefit analysis of international aid reveals unexpected and counter-intuitive risks. An inherent risk is that aid comes at the expense of identity. Identity is undermined in an insidious, cumulative way, first by unwitting dominance and second through unwitting injustice. Hence the problematic in aid and development is not the identity of the aided, but the identity of the aider. Identity is not just an individual, group or institutional entity. It is all three. It has cultural assumptions embedded in its technology, its goals and its means. Becoming aware of the implicit assumptions for which aid is often a standard-bearer is a first step in becoming cross-culturally and cross-contextually more competent. Developing and maintaining such competence is a lifelong and mutual process, for individuals, institutions and groups. This includes organizational groups – the links between them and with the communities they serve. Civil society has a critical role to play in aid and development. It is important for the values and identities of the myriad of aid organizations to be understood, by donor publics, those working in aid organizations, and those who are the recipients and target of aid efforts.

6 | Learning

'The interaction of individuals, possessing different knowledge and different views, is what constitutes the life of thought ... It is of essence that its results cannot be predicted, that we cannot know which views will assist this growth and which will not – in short that this growth cannot be governed by any views which we now possess without at the same time limiting it' Hayek (1944: 181)

'To bring health to a system, connect it to itself ... In order to change, the system needs to learn more about itself from itself. The system needs processes to bring it together ... People need to be connected to the fundamental identity of the organization or community ... to be connected to new information ... to reach past traditional boundaries and to develop relationships with people anywhere in the system' Wheatley (1999)

'The bottom line is that aid agencies ... need to be flexible, "learning" agencies ... in reality, aid agencies tend to be highly centralized with most decisions made at headquarters ... to have rigid programming systems, to use the quantity of funds spent as a measure of the effectiveness of projects and programs while having weak and underused evaluation systems' Whittle and Kuraishi (2008: 467)

In this chapter we argue that understanding the roles that dominance, justice and identity play in international aid is important, but not sufficient. We must also understand that they implicitly shape what and how we learn (or don't learn) from what we do in international aid. Learning from what we do seems such a mundane recommendation! But, in fact, it has been our failure to learn, and often our lack of willingness to learn, which has continually undermined international aid. We begin by considering what learning means in the context of international aid, and the difficulties of sharing that learning between organizations that purportedly have similar aims. We also later consider the discourse of aid in terms of who says what should be learnt. In the debate regarding whether aid should currently be delivered through a 'big push' or more gradually, we argue that change which is incremental – *incremental improvement* – is more likely to enhance ownership and integrity among its beneficiaries. Finally, we consider how both aid organizations and individual aid workers can strive towards a humanitarian work psychology that helps to manage the human dynamics of the aid triangle and so contribute to more effective human development.

Capabilities and justice

We have already stressed, as have others, that 'development' is about a lot more than income or economic growth. The 'capabilities approach' has placed great emphasis on well-being and human development. One of its leading proponents, Amartya Sen, uses the term 'capability', in a broader sense than 'skill' or 'aptitude', as it is commonly used. Instead Sen uses it to refer to the life-paths that are available to people – their actual opportunities – which he sees as their sense of 'positive freedom'. Their 'functioning' reflects the paths they have chosen (from those available to them). While welfare economics traditionally considers factors such as consumption or utility/satisfaction, Sen recognizes that what one 'gets', and how one feels about it, do not neatly project on to a set quality of life. An example he often uses to illustrate this is people with disabilities, who may require different levels or types of resources to provide them with the same 'capabilities' as enjoyed by persons without disabilities (Sen 1985). Our own work on justice, and its interrelatedness to dominance and identity, also chimes with Sen's (2009) most impressive *The Idea of Justice*. One of the key insights that Sen offers in this recent work is that we don't necessarily have to be able to say what is perfectly just, to recognize that some systems of justice are 'fairer' than other systems. Sen's adoption of this pragmatic comparative approach allows for cultural and contextual variations in systems of justice, while also acknowledging the need for some underlying principles of fairness; thus allowing us to note that some systems, including some traditional systems, unjustly privilege certain social hierarchies over others.

Ideally aid and development are associated with increasing people's capabilities. This would include making them less subject to the dominance of others, allowing them to sense and experience justice in their everyday lives and to retain valued aspects of their identity. There must also be an acknowledgement that not all aspects of identity – including traditional cultural identity – are valuable to a person in terms of increasing their 'capability'. For instance, women are treated unequally by many social, employment and justice systems, as are many other marginalized groups. One of the lessons we draw for this book from Sen's recent work is that, similarly, we don't have to be able to define what a singular 'perfect' aid relationship would be like in order to be sensitive to social hierarchies of dominance, the practice of justice and the promotion of dignity and valuing identity.

To address the human dynamics of dominance, injustice and threatened identities does, however, require knowing how and when they come into play and how they might be improved upon. It would be naive to think that all aspects of unfairness can be erased from complex human interactions between more and less powerful operators. It would also be unreasonable, however, not to consider how all organizations involved in aid are implicated in such dynamics, how they can learn from their past experiences (good and bad) and how that learning can be used to improve the effectiveness of aid and its contribution to enhancing the dignity and efficacy of its recipients. We now consider briefly the idea of organizational learning (OL) and how it applies to aid agencies.

Organizational learning theory

A review of organizational learning theory is obviously beyond the scope of our purpose here, and so we seek only to introduce the reader to some key concepts and to think through how they operate in the context of international aid.

Britton defines organizational learning as 'Individual or collective learning in an organizational context that contributes to changed organizational behaviour' (Britton 2005: 56). Thus the organization learns because of what individuals/groups do. This can be contrasted with the 'learning organization', which is an organization that 'builds or improves its practice, consciously and continually devising and developing the means to draw learning from its own and others' experience' (ibid.: 56). In the latter the emphasis is therefore on individuals learning because of what the organization is designed to do. In practice, the idea of organizational learning and learning organizations often go together and are mutually reinforcing. When we talk about organizational learning, we are referring to both processes, unless stated otherwise.

Argyris has contributed one of the most valuable ideas in organizational learning: that people's learning can take place on different planes of awareness. Single loop learning is about approaching a situation in accordance with how it is encountered. Here people 'think inside the box' and deal with the symptoms of problems as they are presented. They ask 'how to' questions and may be able to develop improvements as to how existing rules or procedures work within an organization. This can be very valuable as it may produce more efficient ways of working and/or improve the application of existing procedures. From the aid triangle perspective, however, single loop learning, being more concerned with explicit and operational efficiency, doesn't address underlying human dynamics, but rather the more mechanistic ergonomics or human factors involved in doing a job in a different way to increase productivity.

Double loop learning is about 'thinking outside the box'; it's about questioning assumptions underlying existing rules and procedures and examining the underlying causes of problems, rather than the 'symptoms' they produce. This approach is therefore concerned with developing more effective ways of working, creating new knowledge and insights, developing improved rules and procedures, and developing improved systems and strategies within the organization. From the aid triangle perspective, double loop learning may recognize that there are implicit relationship issues that underlie poor performance and that these issues need to be addressed in more fundamental ways; for instance, by reconsidering the roles that different people adopt.

Triple loop learning is thinking 'about the box', examining core values and rethinking the fundamental purpose and principles of what you are doing. Such thinking may result in a renewed statement of core values and purpose, and indeed a renewed identity for the organization and/or individual. From the aid triangle perspective, triple loop learning involves recognizing that a specific 'problem' in a project may not only reflect the human dynamics of relationship issues, but may also be symbolic of broader discontent with the meaning that is ascribed to the project and its implications for the integrity of those working on it and/or its intended beneficiaries.

If you take the example of stockpiles of food not being distributed in-country during a famine, then an example of single loop learning may be to ask 'What are the barriers to distribution?' Finding out how we can improve logistics to get stuff moved, is therefore the focus. An example of double loop learning may be to ask 'If we want to help people, is the movement of resources to here the best thing to be doing?' It may be that a new distribution centre and different distribution mechanisms are needed. An example of triple loop learning could be asking 'Do we want to "help" people, or "enable" them to cope?' Could we give them money instead of goods and thus try to stimulate the local economy and food production, enhancing their sense of empowerment and control? It may well seem that triple loop learning is 'better' than the other types of learning, but in reality single or double loop learning may well be sufficient to address the problem at hand, and it is not going to be appropriate or practical to examine your core values every time you are confronted with a problem.

A crucial ingredient in loop learning generally is perspective. An old Scottish saying speaks of learning to see ourselves as others see us. A modern-day equivalent is 'perspective taking'. In each case, taking the perspective of 'the other', quite literally, gives a double loop – a fresh perspective on ourselves. We can use our own diagrams to illustrate this process further. Look at Figure 4.2, on double demotivation. An example of single loop learning is when an expatriate aid worker on international remuneration sees only the withdrawal behaviour of a local counterpart, not what lies behind it (a felt injustice, an attempt to restore the balance). A double loop, however, would literally incorporate these feelings and motives, i.e. by leading to an understanding of the reciprocal psychology in the situation. This allows a sort of 'bird's-eye view' of the systems dynamic in play, and confirms that there is more to systems thinking than either perspective alone or even 'one-shot' dual perspectives. Human factors in relationships don't 'freeze' in single frames of inaction; rather they express themselves through dynamic patterns of interaction, continually moving with the time and tide of their context.

In the chapter on justice we questioned how health services are delivered. If we accept that people have a right to health in the same way that they have a right to education, then how can we provide that health for them in resource-constrained environments? One answer, as we have seen, is that, rather than depending on traditional 'Western'-style health providers (doctors and nurses), their tasks can be shifted to new or other cadres of health workers. We need to be open to seeing problems in new ways and learning new approaches to addressing them, even if, or perhaps especially if, these new ways undermine our own position of dominance, our own identity and our own sense of what is right; for instance, that only doctors should prescribe antimalarial medication.

The 'brain drain' and the shortage of resources caused by conflict and natural disasters have meant that many low-income countries have had to think outside the box. For example, in 1980 after the civil war in Mozambique, a shortage of skilled surgeons prompted the government to introduce a new cadre, '*técnicos de cirurgia*' – health workers who were trained (for much shorter periods of time than doctors) specifically to perform surgery. In Tanzania, at independence in 1961, there were only ten local physicians in the country and 420 expatriates who were planning to leave (Mbaruku and Bergstrom 1995). The government took the decision to train assistant medical officers to fill the gap.

Despite evidence that these health workers are as effective as doctors who have received Western-style training, there is a reluctance by some donors to endorse their use; they prefer instead to provide funding to support increased output of doctors and nurses. Accepting this effective task-shifting from doctors to these new cadres does, of course, call into question the skill mix and task configuration, not just of low-income countries' health systems, but also of those in high-income countries. Might this task-shifting have provided a more

TABLE 6.1 A taxonomy of organizational learning

Levels of organizational learning	Process involved in organizational learning	Inputs/outcomes for organizational learning
Individual	Intuiting	Experiences Images Metaphors
Individual	Interpreting	Language Cognitive map Conversation/dialogue
Group	Integrating	Shared understanding Mutual adjustment Interactive systems
Organizational	Institutionalizing	Routines Diagnostic systems Rules and procedures

Source: Adapted from Crossan et al. (1999)

equitable approach to addressing the skill shortage in high-income country health systems? Taking a closer look at organizational learning, Argyris and Schön (1978: 9) suggest:

> There is something paradoxical here. Organizations are not merely collections of individuals, yet there are no organizations without such collections. Similarly, organizational learning is not simply individual learning, yet organizations learn only through the experience and actions of individuals.

Thus, in addition to the different learning loops described above, organizational learning can happen in different ways. Crossan et al. (1999: 525) provide a useful framework for organizational learning, distinguishing between individual learning – through both intuiting and interpreting – integrative learning through groups, and institutionalizing learning through how organizations act. Table 6.1 illustrates the different input/outputs associated with each of these levels of learning. Shifting tasks from one professional group to another will undoubtedly require adaptation not only in practice at the individual, group and institutional levels, but also to our images and symbols that go along with place in hierarchies.

The very idea of 'learning' seems to imply something good. Yet learning can also be wrong! For example, when a situation is mistakenly diagnosed, when inferences are incorrectly drawn, or when lessons are applied in non-comparable situations. Thus learning is much more than listing 'lessons learned'. It is also important to recognize that learning is not a neutral concept; people usually learn for a purpose – be it political, promotional, economic or for some other reason. And so an important question is 'learning for what?'. In our case it's to improve the effectiveness of international aid.

Organizational learning and aid organizations The impetus for improved organizational learning in international aid has come from various sources. Within the NGO/civil society sector these include changes in funding patterns, greater competition for funding, calls for greater 'professionalism' in aid work, a stronger emphasis on the importance of strategic planning and increased expectations of accountability (up and down) (BOND/Exchange 2004). It is argued that increases in aid funding will not help reduce poverty in the absence of major improvements in the quality of aid (Action Aid 2005; Killick 2005). The OECD (2006) notes that 'donors ... could do a much better job at delivering aid more effectively' (p. 4). The 2005 Paris Declaration on Aid Effectiveness, drawn up by over one hundred donor and recipient countries, outlines a series of reforms regarding how aid should be conducted, in order to increase its impact and make achievement of the Millennium Development Goals a more realistic possibility (see ibid.).

There is thus increasing enthusiasm for aid agencies to show they are having a positive impact and to demonstrate that they can learn from both their successes and their mistakes. This drive for accumulating evidence, and basing future practice on that evidence, is a key part of organizational learning.

The Asian tsunami of 2004 was a calamitous and now iconic natural disaster which produced a massive public response of sympathy and donations. Many different aid agencies participated in the response to this event, and much good work was done. But there are also opportunities arising from it to learn from what was not done so well. For example, in some cases there was poor information flow and suggestions of some groups being marginalized: '... there is a serious lack of information about reconstruction flowing to affected communities which is having a material impact on their ability to recover ... Effective strategies for reaching women urgently need to be improved' (UNDP 2005: 2).

One analysis of CARE, Oxfam and World Vision's response to the tsunami found serious flaws. These included failure to recognize the length of time it would take to build permanent housing, and delivery of shelter in India that was 'highly unsatisfactory, with poor sanitation and drainage and high risk of flooding, fire and other hazards' (Bhattacharjee 2005: 24).

In Banda Ache, nine months after the tsunami:

> Great areas of urban landscape remain nothing but rubble, while tens of thousands of people still remain living in tents, which are now rotting with mould; almost half a million people are dependent on food aid. Unresolved land rights, poor coordination and unclear policies still impede recovery ... (World Bank 2005: xiii)

Inter-organizational learning in civil society The base of the OECD's 'aid effectiveness pyramid' is donor-to-donor harmonization, a process whereby donors aspire to be more collectively effective and less burdensome on recipient countries. This is to be achieved through means such as establishing common arrangements, simplifying procedures and sharing information. While the Paris Declaration seeks to change how donors and recipients behave, this also requires intermediaries to participate in the changes and take on board the idea of harmonization (along with alignment, ownership and mutual accountability). NGOs, which often play a mediating role between donors and recipients (Martens 2005), should therefore examine more closely how they can work together to make aid more effective.

Let us briefly consider just one example of how inter-agency competition in the Asian tsunami chimes with some aspects of the aid triangle. Miller (2005) has highlighted the importance of distinguishing between normal stress and grief responses and 'psychopathology'. He notes that 'Asian culture, with its emphasis on group welfare, over individual self-reliance, seems to have been a powerful positive influence' (p. 1031) on how people dealt with the tsunami. In Sri Lanka, which attracted a large number of psychosocial relief agencies, 'At times there were more tents set up for the people trying to help than for the people being helped' (p. 1032). What were the effects of this over-supply of aid? '... NGO's have tried to stake their claims in the refugee camps ... kids get attached to volunteers, and then new groups come and offer incentives for the kids to join their activities instead ... children are torn between these loyalties, and it can be traumatic' (p. 1032).

In terms of identity, it is clearly important for relief efforts to be aware of and give credence to cultural differences in how people experience and respond to particular problems, whether they be a natural disaster, stressful experiences or other difficulties (MacLachlan 2006). While the individualization and the medicalization of grief and stress responses are controversial in themselves, the issue for us here is to recognize that aid agencies did what they could do, even if, in some cases, these might have been the wrong things to do. Thus the identity of tsunami victims, in some cases, may have been a secondary consideration to the exigencies of the aid agencies being seen to be doing something. The need to be seen to be 'doing something' in a major disaster arises because aid agencies are competitors for multilateral and donor-public funding. The need for profile and 'brand recognition' (a dominant position) can subvert the other admirable aims of such organizations.

In terms of psychological and psychiatric problems associated with the tsunami, it seems that pre-existing mental health problems were certainly exacerbated by the situation. Doubtless, new mental health problems did arise too, but unmet mental health needs were much greater prior to the tsunami than after it (Miller 2005).

The need to learn together, for NGOs to share their learning, and to support each other in these activities, would seem obvious. The British Overseas NGOs for Development (BOND) group were among the first to act on this and have drawn up some fundamental principles for facilitating learning partnerships (see Table 6.2).

These recommendations are very good, stressing as they do the importance of power differentials, trust, safety and commitment to learning by organizations. It is also important, however, to acknowledge that OL will not work in the same way in all organizations and that different aid agencies are likely to have different strengths and weakness as regards OL.

More than a decade ago, Edwards (1997: 246) argued that:

NGOs need to develop ways of working that are less focused on promoting their own profile, and more concerned with building alliances, working with others, and dividing up roles and responsibilities in a collaborative way. More openness to new ideas and a greater willingness to learn will be essential in the context of new actors and problems ...

Edwards also recognized that the rapidly changing global context was opening up new possibilities for NGOs to relate to each other in different and healthier ways, fostering the possibility of genuine partnerships (Edwards et al. 1999).

The greater part of published research on OL among international aid NGOs has focused upon OL from an internal perspective (i.e. vertically, or within an organization – intra-organizational learning) rather than from an external perspective (i.e. horizontally,

TABLE 6.2 Principles to facilitate learning in partnerships

1. Fund learning as a core activity	Learning takes time and resources, but forgetting is expensive too!
2. Design projects to explicitly facilitate learning	Learning-related objectives as part of the project work Not just Northern-driven
3. Build on existing opportunities for learning	How to maximize 'on the job' learning; be more systematic; use monitoring and evaluation processes
4. Create safe spaces for learning	Re the threat of change, etc.
5. Develop appropriate systems of measurement and accountability	Including valuing the realities of people 'down the ladder'
6. Build trust and look longer-term	Also, focusing less on short-term outcomes and more on long-term processes
7. Address internal factors of organizational culture	Includes 'shared language, habits, customs and traditions, group norms developed over time, espoused values, skills and shared meanings' (Reeler 2001) – i.e. assumptions. 'As a stabilising force in human systems, culture is one of the most difficult aspects to manage in a climate of perpetual change. The challenge lies in conceptualising a culture of innovation in which learning, adaptation, innovation and perpetual change are the stable elements' (E. Schein 1992: xiv)
8. Recognize and attempt to address power differentials	For example, gender, English

Source: After BOND/Exchange (2004)

or between organizations – inter-organizational learning, through the formation of strategic alliances and networks). The idea of NGO harmonization reaches beyond participating in networks to incorporate much closer working relationships, facilitated by organizations sharing what they know, and how and what they learn. This aspiration challenges the dominance of some players in the aid market over others. We need to understand more about the attitude of NGOs towards sharing their knowledge and learning. Sharing knowledge presents a huge challenge in a market where NGOs are competing for funding against one another. Moreover, knowledge derived through good organizational learning is expensive and may therefore not be readily shared (Grant 1998).

But how strong is the need for such sharing? Are there many different organizations doing similar things in similar contexts? Results of a document/web search of the location and nature of the Africa-based activities for thirty-five members of Dóchas (the Irish NGO umbrella organization) are shown, for 2005/06, in Box 6.1. While Irish NGOs work all over the world, Africa is a particular focus of their activity; as can be seen, up to sixteen different Irish NGOs were working simultaneously in one country, and twelve of these were working on at least one health-related project in the country. If we take into account that this represents the civil society sector of only one (and one very small) country working in one continent, and then contemplate the total number of organizations – international and national NGOs – this represents a staggering plethora of NGO activity, with no doubt some overlap and some potential to share evidence and experiences, and to learn from each other.

In a related study (Forsyth and MacLachlan 2009) we sought to explore the attitudes of senior staff members from ten Irish NGOs, all of whom were members of Dóchas and therefore explicitly committed to learning across the sector. Participants were asked, through key informant interviews, 'What are the strengths, weaknesses, opportunities and threats regarding organizational learning across the NGO sector in Ireland?'

Major strengths of inter-organizational OL included the sharing of information and expertise; NGOs' knowledge of the sector and the sector's knowledge of them; and the collaborative power of

Box 6.1 Reported Irish NGO activity in Africa, circa 2005

Angola – Christian Aid, Concern, Trócaire, WVI

Botswana – Skillshare, VSI

Burkina Faso – Bóthar, Christian Aid, Plan, VSI

Burundi – Christian Aid, CMSI, Concern, WVI

Cameroon – Bóthar, Plan

DRC – Christian Aid, CMSI, Concern, Goal, Oxfam, WVI

Ethiopia – ActionAid, Childfund, Christian Aid, Concern, Goal, Gorta, Plan, Self Help, Trócaire, WVI

Eritrea – Concern, Refugee Trust, Self Help

Gambia – Aidlink, Christian Aid, CIC, Gorta, MWDRC

Ghana – Aidlink, Bóthar, Christian Aid, CIC, Gorta, MWDRC, Plan, VSI, WVI

Guinea – CIC, Plan

Guinea-Bissau – Plan

Kenya – ActionAid, Aidlink, Bóthar, Childfund, Christian Aid, CIC, CMSI, Concern, Goal, Gorta, MWDRC, Oxfam, Plan, Self Help, Skillshare, Suas, Trócaire, VMM, VSI, WVI

Liberia – Concern, Gorta, WVI

Malawi – Aidlink, Bóthar, Christian Aid, CIC, Concern, Goal, Gorta, Oxfam, Plan, Self Help, WVI

Mali – Christian Aid, Plan, WVI

Morocco – VSI

Mozambique – ActionAid, Aidlink, Bóthar, Christian Aid, CIC, Concern, Goal, Refugee Trust, Skillshare, Trócaire, VSI, WVI

Niger – Concern, Goal, Plan, WVI

Nigeria – Aidlink, Christian Aid, CIC, Gorta, VSI, MWDRC

Rwanda – ActionAid, Aidlink, Christian Aid, CMSI, Concern, Gorta, Oxfam, Refugee Trust, Trócaire, VMM, WVI

Senegal – Christian Aid, Plan, VSI, WVI

Sierra Leone – Aidlink, Christian Aid, Concern, Goal, Plan, MW-DRC, Refugee Trust, WVI

Somalia – Christian Aid, Concern, Refugee Trust, WVI

South Africa – Bóthar, Christian Aid, Gorta, MWDRC, Oxfam, Skillshare, VMM, VSI, WVI

Sudan – Christian Aid, CMSI, Concern, Goal, Oxfam, Plan, Refugee Trust, VMM, WVI

Tanzania – Aidlink, Bóthar, Christian Aid, Concern, Gorta, MW-DRC, Oxfam, Plan, Skillshare, VMM, VSI, WVI

Togo – Plan, VSI
Tunisia – VSI
Uganda – ActionAid, Aidlink, Bóthar, Childfund, Christian Aid,
    CMSI, Concern, Goal, Gorta, MWRDC, Oxfam, Plan, Self
    Help, Skillshare, VMM, VSI, WVI
Zambia – Bóthar, Childfund, Christian Aid, CMSI, Concern,
    Gorta, Plan, VMM, VSI, WVI
Zimbabwe – Bóthar, Christian Aid, Concern, Goal, MWDRC,
    Plan, Oxfam, VSI, WVI

NGOs working together. So, for instance, as regards sharing of information and expertise, respondents highlighted benefits to their organization from shared information and expertise in terms of generating funding, being able to develop policies on common issues, determining what proposals were likely to succeed or fail, and logistical matters, such as how to organize visas for overseas travel. Some illustrative quotes from respondents (R) are given below:

In terms of things like best practice, it's good to hear at this level if such and such didn't work, then we can report back and say they're doing that, definitely there's huge learning curves … if someone had submitted a proposal to the Irish government and they rejected [it] for whatever [reason], it's great [to know] so then we don't have to waste the time doing the same thing, so yes, there are huge tangible benefits [to] it. (R6)

… probably be a selfish reason – the recognition of our organization, so we're well known within the NGO fraternity, which is a good thing … We know how to move around but also it's a good information resource … like hearing about funding situations or possible initiatives or things like that. (R7)

[Collaboration confers] enormous strengths in that we can speak with one voice at times, which is very good. I think it just doesn't make sense not to have collaboration. The sector is going to be much stronger when we can come together on certain issues, the 'make poverty history' campaign, for example … Over and above, it makes practical common sense that people who are involved in the same areas of work ... have some opportunity to come together on occasion and have a representative body waving the flag. (R8)

Major emergent themes in terms of weaknesses included NGO limitations, the level of honesty and openness among NGOs, poor OL within organizations, and NGOs having a reactive rather than a proactive approach to their work. Many organizations felt constrained by a lack of human and financial resources, which meant they could not invest as much as they would have liked in linking up with other organizations. Some respondents felt that openness to sharing was sometimes inhibited by organizations wanting to protect their own market and NGO competition for funding; as a result, they were often reluctant to reveal anything that would compromise their market share:

> All charitable organizations, they want the same person's wallet so they are in competition, so like there is only a certain level of, you know, you just don't open the doors and say 'come on in and take away all of my ideas'. (R1)

> I think people are, at the end of the day, protecting their own interests here because it's such a competitive market ... We can learn from each other but there is an element of trust and so long as people's margins aren't affected, they'll share information. It's that simple. (R6)

> Organizations are jealous of their own, or want to keep their own power or economic base. (R7)

> I think there's a tendency ... for organizations, particularly overseas NGOs, to protect what they have and say 'Oh no, we never made a mess here'; big organizations can afford to do it [sharing OL], because they're so big, but anyone else won't do it. (R6)

The reference in the above quote, 'big organizations can afford to do it', again highlights the interplay between dominance and identity. If the NGO is a dominant player in the aid environment, sharing learning is less threatening to their identity. Whereas for smaller NGOs – with perhaps a weaker brand image – there is a greater concern for survival and survival is dependent on attracting funding, which is dependent on positive outcomes, regardless of learning. Much of the behaviour of NGOs in relation to learning is therefore shaped by the funding mechanisms and conditionalities to which they are subjected. If learning is to be encouraged among NGOs it needs to be rewarded as an activity, both in terms of funding the time to do it, and also of affording status to the NGO that reflects on its mistakes, as well as its successes, and makes changes to how it operates as a result of this learning.

Major emergent themes regarding opportunities included collating research, having greater influence over public perceptions of NGOs (branding) and joint fund-raising. Respondents perceived that opportunities were seen with regard to the potential for harnessing research in the sector, which could result in better use of limited resources and increase its professionalism. While some research in this area is being conducted, some organizations professed a lack of knowledge of this work or an inability to easily access the results:

> I think there's huge scope for [research on OL]. Who gathers
> all that, where is all that information, all the theses that people
> like you are doing, where are they? That shared learning is not
> available. There is a huge body of work there that maybe might
> have some use in it … why reinvent the wheel? But also that whole
> research field I think might be something where NGOs could help
> out each other … And that whole thing of research, like all the
> ones in … development studies. Their theses are all sitting out
> there. Who reads them? Who even has a list of them? (R7)

Some respondents cited an opportunity to improve the perceptions the Irish public have of NGOs through Dóchas, which could be a figurehead for the sector and speak on its behalf:

> One of the good things is to see the director getting quoted and
> interviewed on issues affecting all the organizations on whether it's
> legislation or the tsunami, and that's good. Then it looks like we're
> speaking with one voice and if the public feel that the money was
> wasted, you have the director explaining, which is good. (R6)

> I suppose one of the things is the public perception and I'm
> not quite sure if any research has been done on that field. The

perception of the different NGOs. What's the difference between them? Is there any difference? Is it the way they do things – to the person on the street? (R7)

And in relation to the Asian tsunami:

> We could have done an awful lot more in a sense that we could certainly have avoided the over-funding part … the big organizations, they were completely over-funded and that is unfortunate, because other organizations who are much smaller don't have the big budgets to do the marketing to get in those funds, [and they] suffered because there were even less funds for those. (R3)

Finally, one respondent suggested restructuring the sector, so that larger NGOs would work through local NGOs around the country that would already have links with the local population: 'bigger NGOs could be pumping money down to the smaller NGOs and the sector could be supporting itself' (R8).

Major emergent threats were competitiveness, the dangers of over-structuring, non-member NGOs finding themselves on the 'outside', losing out through joint fund-raising, new NGOs taking away from more established ones, and a loss of organizational profile. Competitiveness was mentioned as a possible threat in terms of some agencies losing financially if they gave up too much information regarding their donors or marketing strategies:

> You have to be realistic. It's 2006, we're all in the NGO sector and all NGOs have to be run now in a businesslike fashion … We probably all have the same objective at the end of the day. It's to help the developing world and its people … But it is a business. (R1)

> There is also the element of fund-raising competition between the different groups … There's a lot of flag flying that goes with emergencies, but if you want to raise money for your agency, then it's a means to an end. (R4)

Some respondents perceived there was a threat in not being part of an inter-OL body, resulting in being left out of the information circle, which could be damaging in terms of funding from Irish Aid, and the flow of vital information: 'I think in fact not being part of it is more of a threat because if you look at, say, the Irish government funding, they actively encourage organizations to work together, and I think until we joined Dóchas, they were a little suspicious of us' (R3).

Many of the quotations above reflect remarkably honest and candid views on the pros and cons of sharing organizational learning. This level of openness is to be welcomed, but is not necessarily widespread. Most of the respondents were aware of the success of the Disaster Emergency Committee (DEC) in Britain. Set up in 1963, DEC is an umbrella fund-raising group for thirteen NGOs that has been very successful in raising funds for its members, and thereby alleviating the necessity for its members to raise their own funds. DEC has managed to develop an efficient mechanism for national fund-raising and procedures that ensure a degree of accountability. It has also raised standards regarding how NGOs approach humanitarian issues, and has facilitated coordination and communication among its members.

Several of the more problematic issues noted above concern how cooperation with agencies 'positions' them with regard to the public, government funders and other aid agencies. That positioning is also about perceptions of the relative power and dominance of some agencies over others. As we have seen previously, sense of identity can be threatened by such dominance, and also leads to feelings that others are acting unjustly and 'stealing ideas', even if they are ideas to help others. Thus the idea of inter-organizational learning also brings into relief the aid triangle – dominance, justice, identity – through the process of how agencies relate to each other, and to the broader public, not to mention to the intended beneficiaries of aid.

The tension these findings draw into relief could in fact be quite healthy: the need to compete for funding and to maintain an independent identity may give organizations an incentive to strive for greater efficacy, while greater cooperation could yield potentially large gains. Agencies will need to balance the real benefits of sharing OL – including wanting to and being seen to want to participate in structures that promote good governance – with the need to appear distinctive and independent. This need to appear 'positively distinctive' links back to Figure 5.1 and Tajfel's model of identity differentiation (1978). Yet the manner in which NGOs' performance is assessed for distinctiveness, remains problematic. A narrow focus on short-term targets and time frames, without consideration of the longer-term and possibly more sustainable outcomes, works against cooperation and shared learning.

Some of the reluctance to engage more fully in OL seems to derive from short-term thinking. Engel (1993) argued that members of new networks need to remain committed to overcome the initial organizational and establishment phase, even though there will be no real benefits until the network is established. Our respondents' concerns related mostly to short-term threats, while many of the gains were perceived to be more diffuse and to take longer to materialize. Thus, adoption of a longer-term outlook among members and potential members would lead to recognition that, what helps the sector as a whole, will ultimately benefit its component members.

Practices that bolster trust between organizations would be helpful, and the increasing interest in NGOs working through networks or alliances is encouraging. Alliances offer looser, but more targeted, joint working between agencies to achieve particular goals. In such working arrangements differing (implicit) assumptions about what aid 'is' and what it is 'about' are likely to surface and therefore provoke the opportunity, and indeed the need, for greater reflexivity.

Recognizing complexity

In trying to offer some suggestions for organizational learning we are aware that we are also in danger of oversimplifying the complexity of hugely different contexts and of using our own positions to privilege a particular view of what improving aid might mean. In terms of triple loop learning we therefore want to 'think about the box' that we are in. Any particular development discourse 'orders' the world in a particular way. Thus discourses 'serve to order and regulate the objects of development and, at the same time, serve to demarcate what can and cannot be done and said within development' (Lewis et al. 2003: 545).

Competing discourses are therefore to be welcomed, and this means embracing heterogeneity, interdisciplinarity and hugely varying methods of finding things out. Researchers and academics are not necessarily the best people to do this because their energy, focus and, indeed, ego often get consumed in promoting a rather narrow channel which they can become 'known for' (MacLachlan 2009). The leaders in working with complexity are therefore often not the theorists but the practitioners. But practitioners too can be blinded by persuasive arguments for 'one best way'. Such arguments in themselves may reflect attempts to dominate a discourse.

Robert Chambers warns about the dangers of a single/dominant approach to 'development':

> We must ask: who changes the words we use? Whose language brings forth our world and guides our actions? Who defines what words mean? The world brought forth is usually constructed by the powerful in central places or by those well placed to influence them. The words and concepts of development both express and form the mindsets and values of dominant linguistic groups, disciplines and professions, and organizations. (Chambers 2005: 6)

We recognize that aid and organizational learning is one of those fields where one practice or trend is replaced by a new set of 'buzzwords', often lurking in the 'guise of progress through the manipulation of power relations within the organizational system' (Rhodes 1996: 2). Rhodes also recognizes that 'Knowledge and power are two sides of the same question – something is declared to be true based on the legitimizing power of the person who makes the utterance' (ibid.). This insight also therefore suggests that evidence-based practice and organizational learning are potentially threatening to those who are not 'tooled up' to engage with them, and potentially protective of the larger agencies that can more easily engage them. This, of course, is not an argument against learning per se, but rather about how learning is done and who has the legitimacy to draw lessons from it. Learning may thus imply, and entail, dominance.

While a machinery of organizational learning may therefore privilege the powerful in terms of the scale of NGOs, it may also disempower local practitioners and grassroots knowledge if undertaken inappropriately. Thus David Ellerman of the World Bank argues persuasively that 'If the client is not to be a mug, passively receiving knowledge, then the development organization should not function as a jug, seeking to pour knowledge into the mugs' (Ellerman 1999: 31). Furthermore, 'to impose a model without local learning ... would be to short circuit and bypass the active learning capability of the local policy makers, and to substitute authority in its place' (ibid.: 33).

Conclusion

We have now linked organizational learning to the larger issues of national programmes for change and 'development', and in particular to the controversy concerning how this should be done, who should drive it, how fast it should happen, where the resources should come from, and how sustainable it can be. But how does all this relate to the aid triangle? Identity and learning are closely interconnected. OL promotes a strong sense of identity. The corollary is also true: organizations with weak or fragile identities are likely to resist learning as it represents a further threat to this identity. We believe that shared OL becomes a productive mechanism for addressing the destructive impacts of dominance in the aid world.

7 | Conclusion

In this concluding chapter we briefly consider the implications of the aid triangle for a broader approach to aid. We suggest that human dynamics are easier to consider when change is undertaken incrementally, rather than through the 'large leaps' that characterize some approaches. But we also suggest that incremental improvement does not imply any less ambition, but rather a steadier pace of achieving the necessary improvements in people's lives that we all wish for. While personal awareness is important to facilitate change, it is change at the organizational level in aid agencies which we see as crucial.

Contemporary grand narratives

Green (www.oxfamblogs.org/fp2p/?cat=4) summarizes what he describes as three contemporary grand narratives on aid. He dubs Jeffery Sachs an 'aid optimist'. Sachs's drive, dedication and energy, along with his optimism that poverty can be banished in a generation, cannot be doubted (see, for instance, Sachs 2005). He sees underinvestment in basic services as undermining poor people and sustaining a poverty trap; a trap that can be accentuated by unfavourable geography, as in remote, landlocked or mountainous countries.

Green places William Easterly (2006) in the 'aid pessimist' corner. Easterly is critical of the top-down nature of international aid; its lack of accountability, or incorporation of the experiences of the people it seeks to serve, provides incentives for aid agencies that don't reflect their mission (for instance, measuring funding disbursed rather than poverty reduced). Rather than aid being mediated through top-down 'planners', it should work through bottom-up 'searchers'. Easterly sees these searchers as more grassroots-focused, responding to the local market demands of ordinary people to whom they are accountable and upon whom they are dependent.

Paul Collier (2007) escapes explicit classification in Green's system, but could be called the 'aid trappist': he describes four influential traps that keep people in poverty: conflict, natural resources (having too many is the problem (!), thus attracting exploitative interests), being landlocked and having 'bad' neighbours, and poor governance. He suggests that combinations of aid, increased security (including military intervention), trade policies that are fairer to low-income countries, and appropriate international laws and charters are necessary.

Incremental improvement

One of the explicit issues in the above, and many other, competing approaches to 'development' is the scale and pace of change that we should try for. Psychological, social and cultural change often take longer than does technological change; people need to adapt to the new ways of living that are allowed for by introducing new technologies. And new technologies, or ways of doing things, often have profound implications for local power relations. We have already considered how the origin of ideas – who and where they come from – can reflect familiar patterns of dominance, be seen as unjust by some, and can value the identity and integrity of some groups over others – consider the colonialism and the dynamics of identity struggle depicted in Figure 5.1. Such issues and struggles arise not only at the level of international aid, but also within countries and communities.

Something we may not have given sufficient consideration to, is the situation where an intervention is resisted exactly because it produces a more just situation and, in doing so, undermines the dominance of some groups or individuals over others. As such, it may challenge the identity and status of a local power-broker. An NGO giving free access to medicines that can only be prescribed by NGO staff may, for instance, undermine the status and remove the livelihood of a hitherto highly respected traditional healer. The healer may appeal to a village headman, whose role and integrity may then be questioned unless he can disempower the purveyors of the new initiative.

Intervention programmes are all too often aimed at achieving dramatic changes, the process of which does not take into account, or build upon, the social structures that already exist in a community or culture. While it is tempting to produce sweeping changes quickly, such attempts at change are often unsustainable because they fail to ignite the social forces and institutions that can integrate them into the life of the community. Such an approach sees the strengthening of existing systems as crucial, as opposed to the introduction of systems that work in parallel, sometimes in competition and sometimes in ignorance, with existing systems. An alternative approach, which requires learning from the community, seeks incremental improvement, integrating smaller-scale changes into the sociocultural fabric of community life and into the socio-political systems, both at national and community levels. Social institutions offer vectors for endorsing and supporting change; they need not just be seen as obstacles to such change.

We have previously outlined the principles that support the idea of incremental improvement (Carr et al. 1998; MacLachlan 1996) and the idea that 'the more you change the less you can sustain'; this is because the more you change, the farther you depart from a current supporting social infrastructure. It is, however, the implications of incremental improvement regarding the aid triangle, and for learning in aid programmes, which we want to focus on here. It is clear that knowing what to change, and knowing how to change, are both prerequisites for organizational learning (Barry et al. 2010), and that usually this learning is as much a slow progression of action as it is a gradual accumulation of knowledge.

Often within a community, traditional knowledge, attitudes, beliefs and behaviours reflect an equilibrium between forces, promoting change and forces opposing change. For instance, customs relating to health have evolved, sometimes over thousands of years, in order to serve the well-being of the community and its members. If certain beliefs or practices have existed for hundreds of years, then it is possibly because they are braided into a broader social context that provides social stability. Lewin's (1952) Field Theory describes how a balance exists when forces for change (driving forces) are equal to forces against change (restraining forces). Changing this balance therefore requires either an increase in driving forces or a decrease in restraining forces. According to Field Theory, the first stage of (successful) change involves 'unfreezing', or dismantling, existing patterns of behaviour. In the second stage, 'change', new patterns of behaviour are adopted, hopefully ones that are adaptive to managing the imbalance brought about by the increase in driving forces and/or decrease in restraining forces. The third and final stage, 'refreezing', occurs when people are able to integrate their newly acquired knowledge, attitudes, beliefs or practices into their previously existing repertoire. Lewin's framework is under question in today's turbulent times (Coghlan and McAuliffe 2003). The framework suggests that a) change is linear, and b) a period of change is followed by a period of stability. Because there is little stability in today's world and 'the only constant is change itself' (ibid.: 13), many find Lewin's notion of refreezing, meaning stabilization, to be inapplicable to contemporary organizations. In earlier writings (MacLachlan and McAuliffe 2003), however, we point out that an important feature of Lewin's theory is its explicit acknowledgement that stability reflects a dynamic of interacting forces, not simply a failure of something to happen. This has implications for learning, as we explain:

> Rural peasant communities in many developing countries are sustained through a way of life that may have changed little over hundreds of years. Yet this does not mean that such communities are stagnant. If instead they are seen as a 'successful' balancing act, between opposing forces, then the would-be 'developer' must approach 'community development' with a new set of questions. Instead of asking 'Why have these people not developed more?' a better approach may be to ask 'Why has this situation continued to exist?' and 'What forces are involved in maintaining the balance here?' (Ibid.: 203)

A crucial issue in this whole change process will be the magnitude of change sought. The smaller the change required then the more readily it can be assimilated into the existing repertoire of skills. Imagine the differing degree of change required to adapt to two related messages: 1) 'The way you're treating your child's measles is wrong', and 2) 'Your whole system of understanding health and illness is wrong'.

If members of poor communities are presented with requests to make large changes to their precarious way of life, then their very vulnerability will mean they have much to lose (perhaps including a very meagre income), as well as much to gain. In such a delicate balancing act they may well reject the uncertain (and perhaps familiar) promises of a better life for the relative certainty of a diminished means of existence.

The smaller the proposed change, the less upheaval and adaptation it will require. The problem with this rationale is that, to be realistic, sometimes it is not a small change which is required, but a big change. It may be, for instance, that health practices which were thought to be adaptive at a certain time and/or in a given place are not adaptive in the presenting context. It is suggested that where significant changes in health behaviours are sought, these should be driven through a series of complementary incremental steps in the direction of the desired change. Advanced technology, for instance, often requires advanced and unaffordable maintenance, which often results in premature abandonment when the parts wear out and need replacing (Carr et al. 1998). A broken promise results (Carr 2003). A more incremental improvement philosophy, however, argues for the integrating of new ideas and behaviours into an existing repertoire, prior to the next increment in the change process. Two-wheel tractors (or powered tillers) may be more adaptable and sustainable than larger, more high-tech ones (Francis and Mansell 1988). Of course, the change process is ultimately not directed by the 'expert' as such, but by the ease with which the community can integrate and support new ideas and technologies – the experts learn from the community: alignment. Alignment guides the rate of the unfreezing-change-refreezing process. The practitioner, once having indicated an initial small change, becomes reactive to the community's rate of change. Incremental change is thus respectful of identity.

Incremental improvement is essentially a strategic approach to community change, operationalized through a series of small steps in the desired direction. It is also a learning process for the practitioner, however, because he or she may not know either the best way forward or the ultimate destination of the change process. Ultimately the way in which a community negotiates the change process, through umpteen unfreezing-change-refreezing cycles, is a journey into the unknown. For the development practitioner this uncertainty can be a frustration; so can the slow pace of change. Nonetheless, these may be acceptable costs of a process that can enhance the community's ownership of positive changes (MacLachlan 2006).

The scale and rate of change

There may be an inclination to think that a slow rate of change implies modest change, and a faster rate implies more ambitious change. There are two well-known examples of change that took place relatively slowly but on a very impressive scale. These are Bangladesh's Grameen Bank and BRAC (Building Resources Across Communities). We now draw on the Singapore Management University's (2008) report on these to describe them in the current context. Bangladesh has a population of 144 million people, with about half of them living below the national poverty line. In the last twenty years, however, Bangladesh has actually made quite impressive improvements in human development: in 1990, 10 per cent more of the population was living in poverty than is the case now. An economic growth rate of 4–5 per cent annually and relatively low inflation have contributed to easing poverty, especially in rural areas. The decline in the population growth rate from 2.5 per cent in the 1980s to 1.7 per cent in the 1990s and into the new millennium, and the gains in education – gross primary enrolment increased from 72 per cent in 1980 to 98 per cent in 2001 – are impressive, as is the elimination of gender disparity in primary and secondary enrolment.

In trying to explain this enviable performance, at least in comparison to other poor countries, the World Bank has stressed the role of an active civil society and its strong partnerships with government. Two visionary leaders recently conveyed their experience in this regard in lectures in Singapore: Grameen Bank founder, social worker, economist and Nobel Peace laureate Muhammad Yunus, and BRAC founder and chairperson Fazle Hasan Abed, winner of a Magsaysay award and the 2007 Clinton Global Citizen Award. Their worldwide recognition and acclaim are rooted, at least in part, in ambitious but modest approaches to poverty reduction. For instance, BRAC, initially founded to address short-term crises in Bangladesh in the

1970s, is now a long-term development organization, employing over 97,000 people, one of the world's largest NGOs.

Grameen Bank, also founded in the early 1970s, began by providing grassroots-level loans of $27 to a small village community near Chittagong. The bank, begun as a university project on microcredit, has grown from a handful to 7.31 million borrowers now, 97 per cent of whom are women. Grameen, with nearly 2,500 branches, now provides services to almost 80,000 villages – this constitutes over 95 per cent coverage of all villages in the country.

Grameen Bank's development of micro-finance has also inspired many other similar enterprises across the world. Micro-finance seeks to fill the gap between those living in rural poverty and the more formal financial sector; the sort of collateral required by commercial banks means that, for these banks at least, those most in need of a loan are 'unbankable'. Grameen introduced collective lending and borrowing in small communities, in the absence of physical capital or assets; Yunus facilitated the 'bankability' of social capital to act as a barrier against default – while one person may not be able to pay back a loan in the event of default, a larger number working collectively could. The incentive for repayment was that the money was their own, and defaulting would disbar the entire community from further loans. This kind of 'development' goal can help to bring people together under one objective (termed 'superordinate' or 'interdependent') – qualities that are known to bring otherwise diverse groups closer together in a more cooperative relationship (Carr 2003).

According to Yunus, repayment rates for Grameen Bank average at 97 per cent. This lending had the knock-on effect of promoting a wave of rural entrepreneurship, which significantly contributed to the Bangladesh economy and to the provision of services, to the women's sense of control over their own lives, and their sense of dignity and self-belief.

In 1979 about a quarter of children born in Bangladesh died before reaching their fifth birthday. BRAC volunteers focused on door-to-door education of mothers about diarrhoea – the main culprit in these young deaths – using simple messages and showing the mothers how to make and administer oral rehydration fluids.

Simple but great challenges, such as uncalibrated containers, all of different sizes in different homes, and the need to use only boiled water, were overcome.

With the support of religious schools and the use of novel incentives to gain the trust of men, BRAC had covered 14 million households in 70,000 villages within a decade, virtually every household in Bangladesh, which ranks highest in the use of oral rehydration therapy among low-income countries. BRAC subsequently addressed the problem of poor storage of vaccines leading to spoiling in warm weather, because refrigerators often broke down and took too long to be repaired. BRAC trained a cadre of technicians, who would cycle from village to village, repairing refrigerators. For every 1,000 children born in Bangladesh today, seventy-eight will not survive beyond the age of five, a dramatic improvement on 1979, although clearly still far too many. BRAC's efforts are widely acknowledged to have made a major contribution to this achievement.

Both BRAC and the Grameen Bank promote social enterprises – both for-profit and not-for-profit – that promote the social good. Their 'model' of change is ambitious but their mode of change is often modest. In citing these two examples we are aware that there are also many other success stories in low-income countries, and indeed some of them are larger-scale. In encouraging the value of incremental improvement, we do not wish to negate the possibility of 'large leaps' forward (Carr et al. 1998) but rather to consider the implications of different rates of change for sustainability and for how the change affects people's personal experience of dominance, justice and identity.

Personal transformation and the aid triangle

We are sensitive to the dangers of 'therapizing' aid and development, and suggesting that 'personal work' needs to be done, as well as organizational and community work. This is partly because too great a focus on personal change can detract from the need for broader social activism and social change – it can 'individualize' problems that reside far beyond the individual's reach. Yet if people are not 'cultural dopes' and instead are actively filtering and interpreting ideas that their culture presents to them (MacLachlan

2006), then neither are they 'organizational dopes', only motivated by and only implementing the actions sanctioned by their organizations. Kelman's (1969) distinction between three different responses to change exemplifies the importance of any change needing to be personal, as well as organizational, for it to be successful. One may adopt a change through compliance – that is, through fear of sanction ('if I don't do it the funds will be withdrawn'); through identification (not to be confused with our broader use of 'identity' in Chapter 5), where change is adopted to emulate another individual or cause ('we'll do it because all the other NGOs are doing it'); or through internalization, where change is adopted through a judgement, value or belief that it is a good thing to do ('I'll do it because I really believe it will benefit the community').

The disposition of internalization obviously makes for more sustainable change. Indeed, aid and development work often rely on a level of personal commitment that derives from the meaning that such work has at a personal level. So while we have argued that the aid triangle has relevance at the organizational level, we also want to recognize what this means for the individuals who make up organizations, and the learning that we have argued they need to undertake. If issues concerning dominance, justice or identity resonate for us at an individual level, then it is unlikely that our organizational work is going to be unaffected by them.

Michael Edwards and Gita Sen (2000) have recognized the importance of personal change in this context and developed it in an inspiring paper on 'NGOs, social change and the transformation of human relationships' (see also Edwards, www.futurepositive. org/lovejustice.php). In considering the effects of globalization, they argued that power was increasingly moving from public to private interests and eroding the economic, social and political interests of the majority for the benefit of a tiny minority. They also saw the individualism and materialism of global capitalism as undermining '... the co-operative solidarities and institutions we will need to confront the collective problems that will shape the 21st century ...' (Edwards and Sen 2000: 606). They continue by recognizing that 'We cannot compete ourselves into a co-operative future ...' Instead:

... personal or inner change, *and* social or outer change, are *inseparably linked*. This is as obvious as it is neglected in development thinking, including the praxis of most NGOs. ... We are convinced that any realistic vision of sustainable development must tackle the question of *personal power relations* head-on. (Ibid.: 606, emphasis added)

The global recession has presented us with a unique opportunity to decide whether our system of global capitalism is at a low point in a cycle or at the point of 'reset', where a different form of cooperation and different ground rules regarding dominance, justice, identity and other important issues can be developed.

For Edwards and Sen the interaction of economic power (the distribution of assets and working of markets), social power (the status and position awarded to different social groups) and political power (people's voices in decision-making in both the public and private spheres) produce the 'social order'. Social change then requires a recognition and integration of these modalities of change, because change in one sphere supports change in another. They also recognize, however, that attempts to develop a new social order can also be 'poisoned by the thieves of the heart' (ibid.: 609). These 'thieves', familiar to us all, include personal ego, jealousies, insecurities, privileged positions, nepotism, and wanting to constrain problems within one's own areas of competence, to name but a few. Again, we see these sorts of issues resonating with, and often arising from, concerns with/about dominance, justice and identity – their nudges and tugs, often implicit, are individual concerns that play out in organizational behaviour generally, including aid projects. And, it is important to say, the image (and reputation) of aid organizations play out in how individual members of those organizations treat and are treated by others.

The learning, then, has to take on board the idea that individual and organizational action are inseparable, though many of us – ourselves included – seek solace in constructing the fiction that they are not. In each of our roles we can reflect, particularly at the double and triple loop levels, to what extent we are complicit in dominance over others, procedural or distributional injustices, and undermining the integrity and identity of others. Being the victim of such things is easier and more comfortable to identity than being the perpetrator, so we would be fooling ourselves if we thought that aid and development workers ('do-gooders') were immune from or above engaging in behaviours that diminish others.

Eichler and Burke (2006) have operationalized a key insight – that many biases and prejudices derive from social hierarchies. Thus, sexism and racism interact and interface with other social hierarchies, such as class and sexual orientation. Their BIAS FREE Framework is designed to identify biases that derive from 'any and all social hierarchies'. BIAS FREE stands for Building an Integrative Analytical System For Recognizing and Eliminating InEquities. The BIAS FREE Framework addresses the intersection of biases that derive from hierarchies based on ethnicity, gender, disability, age, class, caste, socio-economic status, religion, sexual orientation, geographical location and immigrant/refugee status, among others, and it considers how these play out in the overall health and well-being of people. The framework is a tool for 'building equitable, more inclusive societies based on respect, equality, human rights and the full participation and benefit of all people' (Burke and Pupulin 2009).

We believe that the BIAS FREE approach can be mapped on to the aid triangle, i.e. how dominance, justice and identity play out on an individual, on a group or organizational level, and indeed on a national and international level. The BIAS FREE Framework is concerned with 'outing' power structures that serve to reinforce and maintain hierarchies. In its use to date, this concerns broader social structures that reinforce the oppression of vulnerable populations. The framework guides users through a rights-based approach to their work, and it promotes the treatment of all people with dignity and respect. The BIAS FREE tool, based on twenty-five years of published research by Eichler and Burke (2006), by helping people to think through the implicit biases through which they operate, could become a key learning tool, both for individuals and for the organizations they constitute.

Whether we think in terms of interventions or research, another aspect of such learning should be awareness that, while we have many 'experts' in different areas of aid, their expertise is too often constrained by a lack of knowledge about just how things are to be done or the ways in which local settings and conditions might influence the response to such interventions. Thus *content* expertise needs to be integrated with expertise regarding the *context* in which the work is to be done and expertise regarding the *process* of service delivery or aid project management (MacLachlan 2009). This book has focused on the latter in particular; on the process skills involved in understanding the human dynamics of development work.

Humanitarian work psychology addresses itself to the fact that much aid and development depends on organizations working well (humworkpsy.org/; see also Berry et al. 2010; Carr et al. 2008). First, it entails promoting what the International Labour Organization (ILO) terms 'Decent Work', meaning work that respects human dignity and freedom. Second, it involves improving work performance for those engaged in poverty reduction, whether that be through promoting health, increasing access to education, or providing opportunities and supports for employment. A central tenet of humanitarian work psychology is that to achieve these goals, organizations must learn. A key precondition for that learning is a meta-awareness of the dynamics of dominance, justice and identity. Humanitarian work psychology views the organizational perspective we have described above as under-appreciated and under-studied, and sees organizations as uniquely intensive human capacitors, for enhancing the capabilities that Sen (1999) calls for (see Carr 2009).

Clearly there may be other frameworks for effectively addressing transformation, both at the individual and at the organization level. The value of the organizational learning concept, and the wider humanitarian framework, is that it situates personal transformation not on the psychotherapeutic couch, but in the cut and thrust of what organizations daily do. While 'individual work' is not to be discouraged, we feel that there is great value in instigating personal transformation through organizational learning practices in aid and 'development' work.

Conclusion

The idea of challenging the status quo has always been daunting; inertia compounded by organizational 'necessities', personal privileges, loyalty to group nepotism and often no little amount of delusional self-aggrandizement conspires to resist change. If we can learn to effectively address, and self-assess, issues of dominance, justice and identity in the process of aid, then we are much more likely to become part of the change we seek. Amartya Sen (2009) reminds us that without a sense of injustice and the desire to do something about it, '... Parisians would not have stormed the Bastille, Gandhi would not have challenged the empire on which the sun used not to set, Martin Luther King would not have fought white supremacy in the "the land of the free and the home of the brave"...' (p. vii). Where aid systems reinforce dominance and injustice, and deprive people of a dignified identity, they can never be considered a means of 'development' and they must be challenged, continually and progressively. All those with an interest in making aid work better need to address these human dynamics, not just as the hoped-for longer-term outcomes of aid, but as a focus of its immediate and deliberate application.

Bibliography

Action Aid (2005) *Real Aid: An Agenda for Making Aid Work*, London: Action Aid International.

Advisory Group on Civil Society and Aid Effectiveness (2008) 'Civil society and aid effectiveness: synthesis of findings and recommendations', 2nd working draft, 16 April, web.acdi-cida.gc.ca/cs.

ADDUP (2009) Final Report to Funders, London: ESRC/DfID.

Agrawal, J. and W. A. Kamakura (1995) 'The economic worth of celebrity endorsers: an event study analysis', *Journal of Marketing*, July.

Allee, V. (2003) *The Future of Knowledge: Increasing Prosperity through Value Networks*, Boston, MA: Elsevier Science.

Angeles, L. C. (2005) 'Capacity building', in T. Forsyth (ed.), *Encyclopaedia of International Development*, New York: Routledge.

Anisya, T. and L. Fritz (2006) 'Disaster Relief, Inc.', *Harvard Business Review*, 14 November, pp. 114–22.

Argote, L. (1999) *Organizational Learning: Creating, Retaining and Transferring Knowledge*, Boston, MA: Kluwer Academic Press.

Argyris, C. (1999) *On Organizational Learning*, 2nd edn, Hoboken, NJ: Wiley-Blackwell.

Argyris, C. and D. Schön (1978) *Organizational Learning: A theory of action perspective*, Reading, MA: Addison Wesley.

Arnold, G. (2005) *Africa: A Modern History*, London: Atlantic Books.

Arnold, T. (2008) The John Kevany Memorial Lecture, 3rd Irish Forum for Global Health Conference, University College Cork, 17/18 October.

Ashman, D. (2000) 'Promoting corporate citizenship in the global south: towards a model of empowered civil society collaboration with business', *Boston Institute for Development Research*, 16(3).

Bandawe, C. R. (2000) *A Schistosomiasis Health Education Intervention among Rural Malawian School Children: lessons learned*, Cape Town: University of Cape Town.

— (2005) *Mind Tips: A Psychology of Practical Living Skills for Malawi*, Balaka: Montfort Media.

Banerjee, A. V. (2007) *Making Aid Work*, Cambridge, MA: MIT Press.

Barber, M. and C. Bowie (2008) 'How international NGOs could do less harm and more good', *Development in Practice*, 18(6): 748–54.

Barbery, C. (2007) 'Response to Banerjee', in A. V. Banerjee, *Making Aid Work*, Cambridge, MA: MIT Press.

Barry, S., L. Hederman, M.

MacLachlan, E. McAuliffe and C. Normand (2010) 'Organisational learning and accountability: opportunity for an Irish contribution to aid effectiveness?', *Trocaire Review*.

Barsky, A. and S. A. Kaplan (2007) 'If you feel bad, it's unfair: a quantitative synthesis of affect and organizational justice perceptions', *Journal of Applied Psychology*, 92: 286–95.

Basu, K. (2007) *Participatory Equity, Identity, and Productivity: Policy implications for promoting development*, World Bank/Conference on New Frontiers of Social Policy, Arusha, Tanzania, Cornell/Harvard University: CAE Working Paper no. 06-06, May.

Berlin, I. (1958) *Two Concepts of Liberty*, Oxford: Clarendon Press.

Berry, J. W. (forthcoming) 'Mobility and acculturation', in S. C. Carr (ed.), *The Psychology of Global Mobility*, New York: Springer.

Berry, M. O., W. Reichman, J. Klobas, M. MacLachlan, H. C. Hui and S. C. Carr (2010) 'Humanitarian Work Psychology: the contributions of organizational psychology to poverty reduction', *Journal of Economic Psychology* (forthcoming).

Bhattacharjee, Y. (2005) 'Indian Ocean tsunami: in wake of disaster, scientists seek out clues to prevention', *Science*, 307: 22–3.

Black, M. (2002) *The No-nonsense Guide to International Development*, Oxford: New Internationalist.

Boggs, L., S. C. Carr, R. B Fletcher and D. E. Clarke (2005) 'Pseudo-participation in communication networks: the social psychology of broken promises', *Journal of Social Psychology*, 145(5): 621–4.

Bond, P. (2006) *Looting Africa: The Economics of Exploitation*, London: Zed Books.

BOND/Exchange (2004) *Learning in Partnerships*, London: BOND (Bond@bond.org.uk) and Exchange (Healthcomes@ healthlink.org.uk).

Britton, B. (2003) *The Learning NGO*, Intrac Publishing, www.intrac.org/publications. php?id=73.

— (2005) 'Organizational learning in NGOs: creating the motive, means and opportunities', Praxis Paper no. 3, INTRAC, Oxford.

Burke, A. M. and A. Pupulin (2009) 'Building an inclusive national strategy for disabled children in Kyrgyzstan', in M. MacLachlan and L. Swartz (eds), *Disability and International Development: Towards Inclusive Global Health*, New York: Springer.

Burt, C. and A. Dunham (2009) 'Trust generated by aid agency web page design', *International Journal of Nonprofit and Voluntary Sector Marketing*, 14: 125–36.

Buzard, N. (2000) 'Information-sharing and coordination among NGOs working in the refugee camps of Ngara and Kibondo, Tanzania, 1994–1998', web.mit. edu/cis/www/migration/pubs/ mellon/2_infoshare.html.

Carr, S. C. (2003) *Social Psychology. Context, communication and culture*, Brisbane: Wiley.

— (2004) *Globalization and Culture: Exploring their combined glocality*, New York: Springer.

— (2009) Keynote: *Poverty Reduction and Paradigm Shift: Yes we can*, Inaugural Symposium on Work Psychology and Poverty Reduction (Humanitarian Work Psychology), University College London, 24/25 June.

Carr, S. C. and C. R. Bandawe (2008) 'Psychology applied to poverty', in P. Martin, F. Cheung, M. Kyrios, L. Littlefield, M. Knowles, J. M. Prieto and J. B. Overmier (eds), *The IAAP Handbook of Applied Psychology* (in submission), Brisbane: Wiley-Blackwell.

Carr, S. C. and K. Coates (2003) 'I/O psychology and migrant selection', 5th Australian Industrial and Organizational Psychology Conference, 26–29 June, Melbourne.

Carr, S. C. and R. O. Rugimbana (2009) 'Marketing and development out of poverty: introduction to the special issue', *International Journal of Nonprofit and Voluntary Sector Marketing*, 14: 95–100.

Carr, S. C., E. McAuliffe and M. MacLachlan (1998) *Psychology of Aid*, London: Routledge.

Carr, S. C., M. MacLachlan, M. Kachedwa and M. Kanyangale (1997) 'The meaning of work in Malawi', *Journal of International Development*, 9: 899–911.

Carr, S. C., M. MacLachlan, I. McWha and A. Furnham (forthcoming) 'Expatriate: local remuneration differences in six cultures: do they undermine poverty reduction work?', *International Journal of Psychology*.

Carr, S. C., M. MacLachlan, C. Zimba and M. Bowa (1995) 'Community aid Abroad: a Malawian perspective', *Journal of Social Psychology*, 135: 781–3.

Carr, S. C., M. MacLachlan, W. Reichman, J. Klobas, M. O. Berry and A. Furnham (2008) 'Organizational pshchology and poverty reduction: where supply meets demand', *Journal of Organizational Behaviour*, 29: 1–9.

Carr, S. C., R. O. Rugimbana, E. Walkom and F. H. Bolitho (2001) 'Selecting expatriates in developing areas: "country-of-origin"' effects in Tanzania?', *International Journal of Intercultural Relations*, 25(4): 441–57.

Chambers, R. (2005) 'Ideas for development: reflecting forwards', IDS Working Paper 238, IDS, Sussex.

— (2008) *Revolutions in Development Enquiry*, London: Earthscan.

Coates, K. and S. C. Carr (2005) 'Skilled immigrants and selection bias', *International Journal of Intercultural Relations*, 29: 577–99.

Coghlan, D. and E. McAuliffe (2003) *Changing Healthcare Organisations*, Dublin: Blackhall Publishing.

Cohen, A. R. and D. L. Bradford (2005) 'The influence model: using reciprocity and exchange to get what you want', *Journal of Organizational Excellence*, Winter, pp. 57–80.

Cohen-Charash, Y. and P. E. Spector (2001) 'The role of justice in organizations: a meta-analysis', *Organizational Behavior and Human Decision Processes*, 86: 278–321.

Collier, P. (2007) *The Bottom Billion: Why the Poorest Countries Are Failing and What Can Be Done about It*, New York: Oxford University Press.

Colquitt, J. A., D. E. Conlon, M. J. Wesson, C. O. L. H. Porter and K. Yee Ng (2001) 'Justice at the millennium: a meta-analytic review of 25 years of organizational justice research', *Journal of Applied Psychology*, 86: 425–45.

Commission on the Social Determinants of Health (2008) 'Closing the gap in a generation: health equity through action on the social determinants of health', Final report, World Health Organization, Geneva.

Cordella, T. and G. Dell'Ariccia (2007) 'Budget support versus project aid: a theoretical appraisal', *Economic Journal*, 117(523): 1260–79.

Creswell, J. (1998) *Qualitative Inquiry and Research Design: Choosing among Five Traditions*, London: Sage Publications.

Crewe, E. and E. Harrison (1998) *Whose Development? An Ethnography of Aid*, London: Zed Books.

Crossan, M. M., H. Lane and R. E. White (1999) 'An organizational learning framework: from intuition to institution', *Academy of Management Review*, 24(3).

Dallmayer, F. R. (2002) 'Globalization and inequality: a plea for global justice', *International Studies Review*, 4(2): 138–56.

Disaster Emergency Committee (2006) 'Tsunami 5 year anniversary', 17 June, www.dec.org.uk/item/386.

Dodson, P. (1998) 'Will the circle be unbroken? Cycles of survival for Indigenous Australians', Discussion Paper no. 12, North Australia Research Unit/ Australian National University (transcript of the 1998 H. C. (Nugget) Coombs North Australia Lecture, Darwin.

Domino, T. M. (2003) 'Toward an integrated communication theory for celebrity endorsement in fund raising', MA thesis, University of South Florida.

Dore, R. (1994) 'Why visiting sociologists fail', *World Development*, 22: 1425–36.

Dumont, R. (1966) *False Start in Africa*, London: André Deutsch.

Easterly, W. (2006) *The White Man's Burden: Why the West's efforts to aid the rest have done so much ill and so little good*, London: Penguin Books.

— (ed.) (2008) *Reinventing Foreign Aid*, Cambridge, MA: MIT Press.

Easterly, W. and T. Pfutze (2008) 'Where does the money go? Best and worst practices in foreign aid', *Journal of Economic Perspectives*, 22: 29–52.

Ecker-Ehrhardt, M. (2007) 'Complex emergencies and symbolic power: the double role of media actors in building and being authorities in a multi-centric world', Paper presented at the German Political Science Association (DVPW), Darmstadt, 13/14 July (also available from ecker@wz-berlin. de).

Edwards, M. (1994) 'New directions in social development research: the search for relevance', in D. Booth (ed.), *Redefining Social Development: Theory, Research and Practice*, London and New York: Longman.

— (1997) 'Organisational learning in NGOs: what have we learned?', *Public Administration and Development*, 17(2): 235–50.

Edwards, M. and D. Hulme (1996) 'Too close for comfort? The impact of official aid on non-governmental organizations', *World Development*, 24: 961–74 (abstract).

Edwards, M. and G. Sen (2000) 'NGOs, social change and the transformation of human relationships: a 21st-century civic agenda', *Third World Quarterly*, 21: 605–16.

Edwards, M., D. Hulme and T. Wallace (1999) 'NGOs in a global future: marrying local delivery to worldwide leverage', Conference background paper, Birmingham, www.gdrc.org/ngo/g-future. html#sum.

Eichler, M. and M. A. Burke (2006) 'The BIAS FREE Framework: a new analytic tool for global health research', *Canadian Journal of Public Health*, 97: 63–8.

Ellerman, D. P. (1993) 'Global institutions: transforming international development agencies into learning organizations', *Academy of Management Executive*, 13(1).

— (1999) *Must the World Bank Have Official Views?*, Washington, DC: World Bank.

Engel, P. G. H. (1993) 'Daring to share: networking among non-government organisations', in *Linking with Farmers: Networking for low-external-input and sustainable agriculture*, Leusden: ILEIA.

Evers, A. and H. Van der Flier (1998) 'Ethnic minorities on the labour market', in P. J. D. Drenth, H. Thierry and C. J. de Wolff (eds), *Handbook of Work and Organizational Psychology*, Hove: Psychology Press.

Ewins, P., P. Harvey, K. Savage and A. Jacobs (2006) *Mapping the Risks of Corruption in Humanitarian Action*, Policy paper, Overseas Development Institute – Humanitarian Policy Group.

Eyben, R. (2005) 'Donors' learning difficulties: results, relationships and responsibilities', *IDS Bulletin*, 36(3): 98–107.

— (ed.) (2006) *Relationships for Aid*, London: Earthscan.

Eyben, R. and R. León (2005) 'Whose aid? The case of the Bolivian elections project', in D. Mosse and D. Lewis (eds), *The Aid Effect: Giving and governing in international development*, London: Pluto Press, pp. 106–25.

Fanon, F. (1961) *Les Damnés de la terre*, Paris: Maspéro.

— (1965) *The Wretched of the Earth*, London: MacGibbon & Kee.

Farmer, P. (2003) *Pathologies of Power: Health, human rights, and the new war on the poor*, Los Angeles: University of California Press.

Ferrinho, P. and W. van Lerberghe (2002) 'Managing health professionals in the context of limited resources: a fine line between corruption and the need for moonlighting', World Bank Working Paper, Report no. 26941, Washington, DC, 1 December.

Festervand, T. A. and J. A. Jones (2001) 'US executives' perceptions of emerging nations as FDI options', *Journal of Business in Developing Nations*, 5, www.rh.edu/lsmt/jbdn/jbdnv501.htm.

Festinger, L. (1950) 'Informal social communication', *Psychological Review*, 57: 271–82.

Forsyth, C. and M. MacLachlan (2009) 'You just don't open the doors and say "Come on in and take away all my ideas": head office attitudes toward inter-organisational learning in Irish non-governmental organisations', *Knowledge Management for Development Journal*, 5: 4–20.

Forsyth, T. (2005) *Encyclopaedia of International Development*, London: Routledge.

Francis, A. J. and D. S. Mansell (1988) *Appropriate Technology for Developing Countries*, Blackburn, Victoria: Research Publications Pty Ltd.

Freire, P. (1972) *Pedagogy of the Oppressed*, New York: Herder & Herder.

Furnham, A. and S. Bochner (1986) *Culture Shock: Psychological reactions to unfamiliar environments*, London: Methuen.

Gauri, V. and J. Galef (2005) 'NGOs in Bangladesh: activities, resources and governance', *World Development*, 33: 2045–65.

Girgis, M. (2007) 'The capacity-building paradox: using friendship to build capacity in the South', *Development in Practice*, 17(3): 353–66.

Glynn, A. and S. C. Carr (1999) 'Motivation and performance in teams: transforming loafing into resonance', *South Pacific Journal of Psychology*, 11: 71–7.

Grant, R. M. (1998) *Contemporary Strategy Analysis*, 3rd edn, Oxford: Blackwell.

Greenberg, J. (2008) *Managing Behavior in Organizations* (5th international edn), Upper Saddle River, NJ: Pearson.

Griffiths, M., H. Mannan and M. MacLachlan (2009) 'Disability advocacy, empowerment and international development policy', in M. MacLachlan and L. Swartz (eds), *Disability and International Development: Towards Inclusive Global Health*, New York: Springer.

Guijt, I., J. Woodhill, J. Berdegue and I. Visser (2003) 'Learning through E-networks and related ME issues', Paper jointly commissioned by Grupo Chorlavi and FIDAMERICA.

Haley, A. and Malcolm X (2001) *The Autobiography of Malcolm X*, Harmondsworth: Penguin Classics.

Hayden, G. and M. Mmuya (2008) 'Power and policy slippage in Tanzania – discussing national ownership of development', *Sida Studies*, 21, www.sida.se.

Hayek, F. A. (1944) *The Road to Serfdom*, Chicago, IL: University of Chicago Press.

Hernandez, S. et al. (forthcoming) 'Mobility and well-being', in S. C. Carr (ed.), *The Psychology of Global Mobility*, New York: Springer.

Hoff, K. and P. Pandey (2004) 'Belief systems and durable inequalities: an experimental investigation of Indian caste', World Bank Policy Research Paper 0-2875, Washington, DC.

Horgan, O. (2000) 'Seeking refuge in Ireland: acculturation stress and perceived discrimination', in M. MacLachlan and M. O'Donnell (eds), *Cultivating Pluralism*, Dublin: Oak Tree Press, pp. 45–69.

Hovland, I. (2003) *Knowledge Management and Organisational Learning: An international development perspective. An annotated bibliography*, London: Overseas Development Institute.

International Civil Society Steering Group for the Accra High Level Forum (2008) 'From Paris 2005 to Accra 2008: will aid become more accountable and effective? A critical approach to the aid effectiveness agenda', www.ccic.ca/.../002_aid_2008-03_summary_paris_2005_accra_ 2008. pdf.

Ivory, B. (2003) 'Poverty and enterprise', in S. C. Carr and T. S. Sloan (eds), *Poverty and Psychology: From global perspective to local practice*, New York: Springer, pp. 251–65.

Jackson, D. J. and T. I. A. Darrow (2005) 'The influence of celebrity endorsements on young adults' political opinions', *Harvard International Journal of Press/Politics*, 10(3): 80–98.

Jackson, J. E. (2002) 'Contested discourses of authority in Colombian national indigenous politics: the 1996 summer takeover', in K. B. Warren and J. E. Jackson (eds), *Indigenous Movements, Self-Representation and the State in Latin America*, Austin: University of Texas Press, pp. 81–122.

Kanyangale, M. and M. MacLachlan (1995) 'Critical incidents for refugee counsellors: an investigation of indigenous human resources', *Counselling Psychology Quarterly*, 8: 89–92.

Katseli, L. T., R. E. B. Lucas and T. Xenogiani (2006) *Effects of Migration on Sending Countries: What Do We Know?*, Working Paper no. 250, OECD Development Centre.

Kellogg Foundation (1992) *Annual Report: Windows of opportunity*, Guildford: Author Press.

Kelman, H. C. (1969) 'Processes of opinion change', in W. Bennis, K. Benne and R. Chin, *The Planning of Change*, 2nd edn, New York: Holt, Rinehart and Winston, pp. 222–30, cited in D. Coghlan and E. McAuliffe (2003), *Changing Healthcare Organisations*, Dublin: Blackhall Publishing.

Killick, T. (2005) 'Don't throw money at Africa', *Institute of Development Studies (IDS) Bulletin Journal*, 36(3).

Krauss, S. I., M. Frese, C. Friedrich and J. M. Unger (2005) 'Entrepreneurial orientation: a psychological model of success among southern African small business owners', *European Journal of Work and Organizational Psychology*, 14: 315–44.

Latham, G. P. (2007) *Work Motivation: History, theory, research and practice*, New Delhi: Sage.

LeMieux, A. F. and F. Pratto (2003) 'Poverty and prejudice', in S. Carr and T. Sloan (eds), *Poverty and Psychology: From global perspective to local practice*, New York: Springer, pp. 147–62.

Levine, R. (2009) *To Rebrand America, Unbrand Aid*, Center

for Global Development: Views from the Center, blogs.cgdev.org/globaldevelopment/2009/10/to-rebrand-america-unbrand-aid.php, accessed 10 October 2009.

Lewin, K. (1952) *Field Theory in Social Science*, New York: Harper & Row.

Lewis, D. (2005) 'NGOs', in T. Forsyth (ed.), *Encyclopaedia of International Development*, New York: Routledge.

Lewis, D., A. J. Bebbington, S. P. Batterbury, A. Shah, E. Olson, S. Siddiqi and S. Duvall (2003) 'Practice, power and meaning: frameworks for studying organizational culture in multi-agency rural development projects', *Journal of International Development*, 15(5): 541–57.

Liebler, C. and M. Ferri (2004) 'NGO networks: building capacity in a changing world: a study supported by Bureau for Democracy, Conflict and Humanitarian Assistance', Office of Private and Voluntary Cooperation.

Lim, A. and C. Ward (2003) 'The effects of nationality, length of residence, and occupational demand on the perceptions of "foreign talent" in Singapore', in K.-S. Yang, K.-K. Hwang, P. B. Pedersen and I. Daibo (eds), *Progress in Asian Social Psychology*, vol. 3, Westport, CT: Praeger, pp. 247–59.

MacLachlan, M. (1993a) 'Splitting the difference: how do refugee workers survive?', *Changes: International Journal of Psychology and Psychotherapy*, 11(2): 155–8.

— (1993b) 'Sustaining human resource developments in Africa: the influence of expatriates',

Management Education and Development, 24(2): 167–71.

— (1996) 'From sustainable change to incremental improvement: the psychology of community rehabilitation', in S. C. Carr and J. F. Schumaker (eds), *Psychology and the Developing World*, Westport, CT: Praeger, pp. 26–37.

— (2002) 'Die Arbeit mit Psychotrauma: Personliche, kuterelle and kontextuelle Probleme' [Working with psychotrauma: personal, cultural and contextual reflections], in K. Ottomeyer and K. Peltzer (eds), *Uberleban am Abgrund: Psychotrauma und Menschenrechte*, Klagenfurt/Celovec: Drava Verlag, pp. 231–44.

— (2006) *Culture and Health: A Critical Perspective towards Global Health*, 2nd edn, Chichester: Wiley.

— (2009) 'Rethinking global health research: towards integrative expertise', *Globalisation and Health*, 5(6).

MacLachlan, M. and S. C. Carr (1994) 'Pathways to a psychology for development: reconstituting, restating, refuting and realising', *Psychology and Developing Societies*, 6(1): 21–8.

— (2005) 'The human dynamics of aid', *OECD Policy Insights*, 10, www.oecd.org/dev/insights.

MacLachlan, M. and E. McAuliffe (2003) 'Poverty and process skills', in S. C. Carr and T. Sloan (eds), *Poverty and Psychology: Critical Emergent Perspectives*, Boston, MA: Kluwer/Plenum.

MacLachlan, M. and L. Swartz (2009) (eds) *Disability and International Development: Towards*

Inclusive Global Health, New York: Springer.

MacLachlan, M., S. C. Carr and I. McWha (eds) (2008) *Interdisciplinary Research for Development: A Workbook on Content and Process Challenges*, New Delhi: GDN.

Mahroum, S. (2000) 'High skilled globetrotters: mapping the international migration of human capital', *R & D Management*, 30: 23–32.

Manafa O., E. McAuliffe, F. Maseko, C. Bowie, M. MacLachlan and C. Normand (2009), 'Retention of health workers in Malawi: perspectives of health workers and district management', *Human Resources for Health*, 7(65), 28 July.

Manning, R. (2006) 'Technical cooperation', *Development Assistance Committee Journal*, 7: 111–38.

Marin, M. del Pilar Uribe (1998) 'Oxy in U'wa territory: the announcement of a possible death', *Indigenous Affairs*, 1: 56–61.

Marmot, M. (2008) 'The Report of the Commission for the Social Determinants of Health', Global Ministerial Forum on Research for Health, Bamako, 17–19 November.

Martens, B. (2005) 'Why do aid agencies exist?', *Development Policy Review*, 23(6): 643–63.

Maxwell, S. (2004) Comments at OECD Workshop on the Future of International Aid.

Mbaruku, G. and S. Bergstrom (1995) 'Reducing maternal mortality in Kigoma, Tanzania', *Health Policy and Planning*, 10: 71–8.

McAuliffe, E. and M. MacLachlan (2005) 'Turning the ebbing tide: knowledge flows and health in low-income countries', *Higher Education Policy*, 18: 231–42.

McAuliffe, E., O. Manafa, F. Maseko, C. Bowie and E. White (2009a) 'Understanding job satisfaction amongst mid-level cadres in Malawi: the contribution of organisational justice', *Reproductive Health Matters*, 17(33): 80–90.

McAuliffe, E., O. Manafa, C. Bowie, L. Makoae, F. Maseko, M. Moleli and D. Hevey (2009b) 'Managing and motivating: pragmatic solutions to the brain drain', Chapter in S. Kebane, *Human Resources in Healthcare, Health Informatics and Health Systems*, IGI Global.

McAuliffe, E., C. Bowie, O. Manafa, F. Maseko, M. MacLachlan, D. Hevey, C. Normand and M. Chirwa (2009c) 'Measuring and managing the work environment of the mid-level provider – the neglected human resource', *Human Resources for Health*, 7(13).

McMaster, J. (2008) 'Direct budget support versus project aid', in M. MacLachlan, S. C. Carr and I. McWha (eds), *Interdisciplinary Research for Development: A Workbook on Content and Process Challenges*, New Delhi: GDN.

McWha, I. (forthcoming) 'The roles of, and relationships between, expatriates, volunteers, and local development workers', *Development in Practice*.

McWha, I. and M. MacLachlan (forthcoming) 'Exploring relationships between workers in organisations focused on poverty reduction', *Journal of Manage-rial Psychology*.

Mendelson, S. F. and J. K. Glenn (2002) (eds) *The Power and Limits of NGOs*, New York: Columbia University Press.

Miller, G. (2005) 'The tsunami's psychological aftermath', *Science*, 309: 1030–33.

Ministry of Finance (2004) *Poverty Eradication Action Plan (2004/4–2007/83)*, Government of Uganda, Kampala: MFPED.

Mji, G., S. Gcagaj, N. Melling-Williams and M. MacLachlan (2009) 'Disability Networking for Development: Introducing the African Network for Evidence to Action on Disability (AfriNEAD)', in M. MacLachlan and L. Swartz (eds), *Disability and International Development*, New York: Springer.

Moore, M. (2001) *Political Under-development: What causes bad governance*, Brighton: Institute of Development Studies.

— (2007) 'Response to Banerjee', in A. V. Banerjee, *Making Aid Work*, Cambridge, MA: MIT Press.

Moscovici, S. (1976) *Social Influence and Social Change*, London: Academic Press.

Moyo, D. (2009) *Dead Aid: Why aid is not working and how there is another way for Africa*, London: Allen Lane.

Nyerere, J. (1968) *Freedom and Socialism. A Selection from Writings and Speeches, 1965–1967*, Dar es Salaam: Oxford University Press.

Obama, B. (2007) *Dreams from My Father: A story of race and inheritance*, Edinburgh: Canongate Books.

ODI (2006) 'Reforming the international aid architecture: options and ways forward', Working Paper 278, Overseas Development Institute, London.

OECD (2006) 'Aid effectiveness: three good reasons why the Paris Declaration will make a difference', 2005 Development Co-Operation Report, 7(1).

Offenheiser, R. C. and D. Jacobs (2007) in A. V. Banerjee, *Making Aid Work*, Cambridge, MA: MIT Press, Cambridge.

Onunaiju, C. (2009) 'Questions about the United Nations', *Daily Trust*, 19 October.

Pasteur, K. and P. Scott-Villiers (2006) 'Learning about relation-ships in development', in R. Eyben (ed.), *Relationships for Aid*, London: Earthscan.

Ping-Ngoh Foo., J. and J. Chein-Hsing Sung (2002) 'The impact of governance obstacles and state capture of transition countries on Foreign Direct Investment', *Journal of Business in Developing Nations*, 6: 1–27.

Provan, K. G., J. M. Beyer and C. Kruytbosch (1980) 'Environ-mental linkages and power in resource-dependence relations between organisations', *Administrative Science Quar-terly*, 25(2): 200–225.

Pyszczysnki, T., S. Solomon and J. Greenberg (2003) *In the Wake of 9/11: The Psychology of Terror*, Washington, DC: American Psychological Associ-ation.

Rapadas, J. M. (2007) 'Transmis-sion of violence: the legacy of colonialism in Guam and the path to peace', *Journal of Pacific Rim Psychology*, 1:

33–40 (special issue dedicated to indigenous healing).

Reeler, D. (2001) *Unlearning – Facing Up to the Real Challenge of Learning*, South Africa: CDRA, www.cdra.org.za/Publications, accessed July 2003.

Rhodes, C. (1996) 'Researching organisational change and learning: a narrative approach', *The Qualitative Report*, 2(4).

Rocha Menochal, A. and A. Rogerson (2006) 'Which way the future of aid? Southern civil society perspectives on current debates on reform to the international aid system', Working Paper 259, Overseas Development Institute, London.

Rodney, W. (1972) *How Europe Underdeveloped Africa*, London: Bogle L'Ouverture Publications.

Rosenfield, S. A. (2004) *Networking for Learning: What Can Participants Do?*, Interchurch Organisation for Development Cooperation (ICCO), Zeist: European Centre for Development Policy Management.

Ryles, J. (1998) *Dispatches from Disaster Zones: The reporting of humanitarian emergencies*, London: Church House.

Sachs, J. (2005) *The End of Poverty: Economic Possibilities for Our Time*, New York: Penguin Press.

Samman, E., E. McAuliffe and M. MacLachlan (2009) 'The role of celebrity in endorsing poverty reduction through international aid', *International Journal of Nonprofit and Voluntary Sector Marketing*, 14: 137–48.

Sánchez, E., K. Cronick and E. Wiesenfeld (2003) 'Poverty and community', in S. C. Carr and T. S. Sloan (eds), *Poverty and Psychology: From global perspective to local practice*, New York: Springer, pp. 123–45.

Schein, E. (1990) 'Organizational culture', *American Psychologist*, 45: 109–19.

— (1992) *Organizational Culture and Leadership*, 2nd edn, San Francisco, CA: Jossey-Bass.

Schein, V. (1999) 'Poor women and work in the Third World: a research agenda for organizational psychologists', *Psychology and Developing Societies*, 11: 105–17.

— (2003) 'The functions of work-related group participation for poor women in developing countries: an exploratory look', *Psychology and Developing Societies*, 15: 123–42.

Scisleski, A. C. C., C. Maraschin and J. Tittoni (2006) 'The social psychology of the work in communities: limits and possibilities', *Revista Interamericana de Psicologia*, 40: 51–8 (Spanish, abstract only).

Segal, R. (1966) *The Race War*, London: Jonathan Cape.

Selmer, J. (forthcoming) 'Cross-cultural training and global mobility', in S. C. Carr (ed.), *The Psychology of Global Mobility*, New York: Springer.

Sen, A. (1985) *Commodities and Capabilities*, MO: Elsevier Science Ltd.

— (1999) *Development as Freedom*, Oxford: Oxford University Press.

— (2000) *Freedom, Rationality, and Social Choice: The Arrow Lectures and Other Essays*, Oxford: Oxford University Press.

— (2009) *The Idea of Justice*, London: Allen Lane.

Senge, P. M. (2002) 'Creating the world anew', *The Systems Thinker*, 13(3): 2–6.

Sherif, M. (1936) *The Psychology of Social Norms*, New York: Harper.

Sidanius, J. and F. Pratto (1999) *Social Dominance: An Intergroup Theory of Social Hierarchy and Oppression*, New York: Cambridge University Press.

Sidanius, J., F. Pratto, C. van Laar and S. Levin (2004) 'Social dominance theory: its agenda and method', *Political Psychology*, 25: 845–80.

Singapore Management University (2008) *A Tale of Two NGOs: Bangladesh's Grameen Bank and BRAC*, 4 February, knowledge.smu.edu.sg/article.cfm?articleid=1116.

Singer, P. (2008) *The Life You Can Save: Acting now to end world poverty*, New York: Random House.

Slim, H. (2003) 'Argument and method in humanitarian persuasion', Presented at the Humanitarian Negotiators Network, 12–14 May, Talloires (available from the Centre for Humanitarian Dialogue, www.hdcentre.org).

Smyth, C., M. MacLachlan and A. Clare (2003) *Cultivating Suicide? Destruction of self in a changing Ireland*, Dublin: Liffey Press.

Tajfel, H. (1978) *Differentiation between Social Groups*, London: Academic Press.

Tepper, B. J. (2001) 'Health consequences of organizational injustice: tests of main and interactive effects', *Organizational Behaviour and Human Decision Processes*, 86: 197–215.

Thibaut, J. W. and H. H. Kelley (1959) *The Social Psychology of Groups*, New York: Wiley.

Tsang, E. W. K. (1997) 'Organisational learning and the learning organisational: a dichotomy between descriptive and prescriptive research', *Human Relations*, 50: 73–89.

UNDP (1997) *Capacity Development. Technical Advisory Paper 2*, New York: United Nations Development Programme.

— (2005) '"Where's my house?" Improving communication with beneficiaries: an analysis of information flow to tsunami affected populations in Aceh Province', Based on research by the UN-OCHA Public Information Working Group.

Ungerer, C. (2007) 'Influence without power: middle powers and arms control diplomacy during the Cold War', *Diplomacy and Statecraft*, 18: 393–414.

United Nations (2003) *Millennium Development Goals: A Compact among Nations to End Human Poverty*, UNDP, New York: Oxford University Press.

Van Knippenberg, D. (2000) 'Work motivation and performance: a social identity perspective', *Applied Psychology: An International Review*, 49: 357–71.

Vasquez, I. (2007) 'Comment', in A. V. Banerjee (ed.), *Making Aid Work*, Boston, MA: MIT Press.

Vestergaard, A (2008) 'Humanitarian branding and the media: the case of Amnesty International', *Journal of Language and Politics*, 7: 471–93.

Walpole, S. (2007) 'Research is power', in *Young Voices in Research for Health*, Geneva:

Global Forum for Health Research, www.globalforum health.org.

Watkins, B. (2006) *Humanitarian Practice Network*, www.odihpn. org/report.asp?ID=2353, accessed 10 February 2007.

Werker, E. and F. Z. Ahmed (2008) 'What do non-governmental organizations do?', *Journal of Economic Perspectives*, 22: 73–92.

Wheatley, M. J. (1999) *Leadership and the New Science: Discovering Order in a Chaotic World*, 2nd edn, San Francisco, CA: Berrett-Koehler.

Whittle, D. and M. Kuraishi (2008) 'Competing with central planning: marketplaces for international aid', in W. Easterly (ed.), *Reinventing Foreign Aid*, Cambridge, MA, pp. 461–84.

Wiewel, W. and A. Hunter (1985) 'The interorganizational network as a resource: a comparative case study on organisational genesis', *Administrative Science Quarterly*, 30(4): 482–96.

Wilkinson, R. and K. Pickett (2009) *The Spirit Level: Why more equal societies almost always do better*, London: Allen Lane.

Willits-King, B. and P. Harvey (2005) *Managing the Risks of Corruption in Humanitarian Relief Operations*, Study for the Department for International Development, Overseas Development Institute – Humanitarian Policy Group.

Worchel, S., H. Rothgerber, E. A. Day, D. Hart and J. Butemeyer (1998) 'Social identity and individual productivity within groups', *British Journal of Social Psychology*, 37: 389–413.

World Bank (2005) *Aceh and Nias One Year after the Tsunami: The Recovery Effort and Way Forward*, Nias: Badan Rehabilitasi dan Rekonstruksi NAD-Nias.

— (2009) *Governance and Anti-Corruption*, web.worldbank. org/wbsite/external/wbi/wbi programs/psglp/0„menuPK: 461645~pagePK:64156294~piPK :64156292~theSitePK:461606,00. html, accessed 12 October 2009.

Yiu, L. and R. Saner (2005) *Decent Work and Poverty Reduction Strategies (PRS): An ILO Advocacy Guidebook*, Geneva: International Labour Organization.

Index

Abed, Fazle Hasan, 16, 146
aboriginal peoples, 88, 93, 96,
    99–100
absenteeism, of health workers, 61
accountability, 33, 34–5, 37–8, 63,
    137, 141
Advisory Group on Civil Society
    and Aid Effectiveness, 110–11
advocacy skills: demand for, 104;
    importance of, 103
affirmative action, 93
Africa, poverty in, 19, 41
African Forum and Network
    on Debt and Development
    (AFRODAD), 20
African Policy on Disability and
    Development (APODD), 104
Agrawal, J., 40
Ahmed, F. Z., 107, 108, 109,
    112–13
aid: at the expense of identity, 117;
    effectiveness of, 79; failure of,
    10; fungibility of, 32; global
    totals of, 108; idea of, 10–16;
    ineptness of, 23; over-supply
    of, 128; political economy of,
    16–19; purpose of, 20; relation
    to development, 11–22
aid agencies, rationale of, 107–8
aid industry, 18
aid optimism/pessimism, 141
aid systems, incorporate power
    relationships, 3
aid workers: salaries of, 26–7, 37,
    43, 53; status of, 53
alignment, 145; principle of, 84
Anisya, T., 115
Antares Foundation, 8
Argyris, C., 122, 126
Arnold, G., 17, 18

Arnold, Tom, 113
Australia, 96, 99–100; as *terra
    nullius*, 90

Banda Ache, effects of tsunami in,
    127
Bandawe, C. R., 83
Banerjee, Abhijit, 24–5, 30
Bangladesh, development in, 146
Barber, M., 112
Basu, Kaushik, 87, 93
Becker, Ernest, 81–2
Berlin, Isaiah, *Two Concepts of
    Liberty*, 83
BIAS FREE Framework, 151
Black, M., 10
'black is beautiful' movement, 93
Bolivia: aid project in, 108;
    democracy project in, 97
Bond, Patrick, 19
Bono, 2, 39, 41
Bowie, C., 112
brain drain, 47, 52, 124
brain waste, 48, 52
brand aid, 114–17
brand competition, 117
brand recognition, 116; of aid
    agencies, 129, 135
British Airways, 116
British Overseas NGOs for
    Development (BOND), 129
Britton, B., 121
budget support, direct, 30–2
Building Resources Across
    Communities (BRAC), 16, 146–8
Burke, Mary Anne, 151

Calderisi, Robert, 11
capabilities, and justice, 120–1
capacity building, 98–100

capacity development, use of term, 98
CARE, 107, 127
Carr, S. C., 52
caste system in India, 91–2
Catholic Relief Services organization, 107
celebrity, as dominance, 38–43
Celebrity Coalition, 40
celebrity recognition, 114
Celtic Tiger phenomenon, 5
Chambers, Robert, 139
change: incremental *see* incremental change; scale and rate of, 146–8
child mortality, in Bangladesh, 147–8
civil society, 118; identity and, 106–14; role of, 146
Clinton, Bill, 15
Clooney, George, 39
Coates, K., 52
Coghlan, D., 55
Collier, Paul, 10, 142
Commission for Africa, 19
Commission on the Social Determinants of Health, 59
complexity, recognition of, 138–40
Concern Worldwide, 113
conditionalities of aid, 30, 38
condoms, supplying of, 109
coping strategies of workers, 71–6
corruption, 34–7, 60–1, 64–5, 86; positive aspects of, 70
Cowell, Alan, 40
Crossan, M. M., 126
cultural difference, 56
cultural training, 104–5

Dar es Salaam, University of, 44
Darrow, T. I. A., 40
death, managing fear of, 82
'Decent Work', 103, 152
deference, 29
demotivation, 72, 74, 76; double, 77, 95
Department for International Development (DfID), 71

dependence on aid, 18, 52, 80
Descartes, René, 84
development: concepts of, 4–6, 139; inclusive, 21–2; people-centred, 7; relational, 6–7; unevenness of, 21
Diana, Princess, 41
differentials in remuneration, 76, 95
dignity, 85, 152
Direct Budget Support (DBS), 37
Disaster Emergency Committee (DEC), 137
dissent, legitimation of, 14
Dóchas organization, 131, 135, 137
Dodson, Pat, 80, 93, 95, 96
dominance, 7–8, 12, 22–58, 114, 149; against individuals, 47–51; celebrity as, 38–43; in institutions, 44–7; in organizations, 43–4; priming of, 52–3
drugs, reselling of, 61
dual salary, concept of, 78
Dumont, René, 10

East African Community (EAC), 44
Easterly, William, 11, 108, 141; *The White Man's Burden*, 23
Ecker-Ehrhardt, M., 116
Economic and Social Research Council (ESRC), 71
Edwards, Michael, 23, 129, 149–50
Eichler, Margarit, 151
Ellerman, David, 140
Emergency Plan for AIDS Relief, 114
empowerment, 21, 22; through aid, 3, 4
Engel, P. G. H., 138
entertainers, involved with aid, 38–9
entrepreneurship, 19; orientation towards, 87
equality, of resources, 62–3
Ewins, P., 36
exclusion, 91–3
expatriates, 56, 78; as symbols, 80; guilt of, 73, 74, 75, 76; hiring of, 45–6; remuneration of, 53, 72,

73, 76; sense of superiority of, 73; status of, 43
expatrocracy, 54–5
experts, confused with expats, 4
extended families, in Africa, 72
Eyben, Rosalind, 97–8

fairness, 62; of justice systems, 120
Fanon, Frantz, 91, 96; *Black Skin, White Masks*, 29
Farmer, Paul, 11
fee-splitting among health workers, 61
Feed the Children, 107
Ferrinho, P., 61, 68
field theory, 143–4
Food for the Poor, 107
Ford Foundation, 108
forgetting the past, 85
Freire, Paulo, 104
Freud, Sigmund, 82
Fritz, L., 115
functionality, 65–6

Galef, J., 112
Gandhi, Mohandas Karamchand, 16, 153
Gates Foundation, 108
Gauri, V., 112
Geldof, Bob, 2, 39, 41
Glenn, J. K., 111
Global Development Network, 15
Global Fund to Fight HIV/AIDS, Tuberculosis and Malaria, 20
Global Health Initiative (USA), 20
governance, 37–8, 86; good, 34, 60
governments, undermining authority of, 33, 38
Grameen Bank, 146–8; repayment rates, 147
Group of 8 (G8), 46

Hancock, Graham, 11
harmonization, 110
Hayek, Friedrich von, 119
health, as driver of economic growth, 14–15

health care, 60; delivery of, 124; skills shortages in, 124
health workers: coping strategies of, 61; distribution of workloads among, 68
hero-innovator, narrative of, 28
hierarchy, 25–6, 30, 52, 56, 57, 69, 151
HIV/AIDS, 33
Hoff, K., 91–2
Hollywood, 40
homo dominicus, 23, 58
Human Development Index, 52
human dynamics of development work, 152
human relationships, transformation of, 149
humanitarian work psychology, 152
Huntington Institute, 8

identity, 3, 7–8, 12, 80–118, 121, 149; and civil society, 106–14; cultural, 106; differentiation of, 138; group identity, 83–6; individual, 86–9; institutional, 86
identity cards for rag-pickers, 101, 102
immigrants, exclusion of, 105
immortality, 82
inclusion, 90–1
incremental change, 120, 141, 142–6
India: economic growth of, 14; growing confidence in, 86
injustice, 3, 12
institutions, dominance in, 44–7
intellectual dominance, 25
International Civil Society Steering Group for the Accra High Level Forum, 110
International Labour Organization (ILO), 103, 152
International Monetary Fund (IMF), 19
interorganizational learning, 128–38
investor confidence, 86
Ireland, economic growth of, 5, 34
Ivory, B., 99

Jackson, D. J., 40
Jacobs, D., 59
job satisfaction, 66, 67
Jolie, Angelina, 41
justice, 7–8, 59–79, 149; distributive,
    62–3, 66–7, 72; fairness of,
    120; in the workplace, 66;
    informational, 65; interactional,
    64–5, 66; procedural, 63–4, 67;
    restorative, 93, 96; taxonomy of,
    70; types of, 62
justice restoration theory, 72
justice theory, 76

Kamakura, W. A., 40
Kellogg Foundation, 108
Kelman, H. C., 149
Kim, Jim Yong, 11
King, Martin Luther, 153
Kuraishi, M., 119

Latham, G. P., 59
learning, 151; from communities,
    145; in context of aid, 119–40; in
    partnerships, 130; organizational
    see organizational learning
learning organization, 121–2
legitimating myths, 28
León, Rosario, 97–8
Lerberghe, W. van, 61, 68
Lesotho, healthcare in, 109–10
Levine, R., 114
Lewin, K., 143–4
Lim, A., 51
literacy, 102; classes, 100–1
loop learning: double, 122, 123;
    single, 122; triple, 122–3, 138
low-income country, use of term,
    5–6

MacLachlan, M., 80
Malawi: drought in, 94; National
    University of, 73; study of health
    workers in, 37, 61, 66, 68, 77,
    110
Malcolm X, 90, 96
Maren, Michael, 11

Marmot, M., 59
Martens, Bertin, 107–8
Maxwell, Simon, 15
McAuliffe, E., 55
McManus, J. P., 2
McMaster, J., 32
Médecins sans Frontières, 117
Mellon, Niall, 2
Mendelson, S. F., 111
micro-credit, 147; access to, 101; in
    Bangladesh, 112; in Nicaragua,
    84
migration–development nexus,
    47–8, 51
Millen, Joyce, 11
Millennium Challenge Account, 114
Millennium Development Goals,
    103, 127
moonlighting by workers, 61, 63,
    65, 69
Moore, M., 23, 38, 80
Moyo, Damisa, 10, 11, 38–9
Mozambique, health workers in,
    124

Nankani, Gobind, 15
Narayan, Laxmi, 101–2
neoliberalism, 13
nepotism, 64–5
Netherlands: awareness-raising
    programmes in, 51; job selection
    panels in, 55
New Zealand, bias against migrants
    in, 48–51
NGO-ization of international aid,
    116
Nigeria, member of Security
    Council, 47
non-governmental organizations
    (NGOs), 33–4, 57, 77, 116,
    129, 142, 147, 149; active in
    Africa, 132–3; as middlemen
    of aid industry, 108; as part of
    problem, 107; as subgroup of
    civil society, 107; collaborative
    power of, 133; competition
    between, 136 (for funding,

131, 134); criticism of, 111–13; distinct identities of, 109; funding model of, 109; growing numbers of, 113; harmonization of, 131; idealization of, 108; in Bangladesh, 109; in Ireland, 131; in Uganda, 109; networking of, 138; reactive approach of, 134; relevant to identity, 106

Obama, Barack, 20, 114; *Dreams from My Father*, 87
Offenheiser, R. C., 59
Office of Aboriginal Development, 98
Onunaiju, C., 47
oral rehydration, 148
O'Reilly, Anthony, 2
Organisation for Economic Co-operation and Development (OECD), 127, 128; Development Assistance Committee (DAC), 19
organizational learning, 140, 152; and aid organizations, 126–8; sharing of, 137; theory, 121–38
organizations, dominance in, 43–4
over-funding of organizations, 136
ownership: of aid, 115; of projects, 97
Oxfam, 1, 59, 102, 116, 117, 127; critique of, 114
Oxfam Australia, rag-pickers' project, 100–1
Oxfam UK, declines aircraft trips, 115

Pandey, P., 91–2
Papua New Guinea, 77–8
Paris Declaration on Aid Effectiveness, 78, 84, 111, 127, 128
participation, 21, 106
participative equity, 87
pay differentials, 74
'pay me' reaction, 94–5, 98
People in Aid, 8
personal transformation, 148–52

perspective sharing, 123
philanthropy, 2–3
Pickett, K., 59
pop culture of aid, 38
poverty, reduction of, 21, 27, 41, 42, 57, 60, 103, 126, 146
Poverty Reduction Strategy Papers (PRSPs), 63, 104
poverty trap, 142
power: distribution of, 60; roots of, 26
power structures, outing of, 151
pre-departure training, 77
primary commodities, production of, 18
Project ADDUP, 70–1, 75–6, 77, 78
project aid, 30–2, 65, 70–1
project monitoring, 35

rag-pickers, in India, 100–3, 105
Rank, Otto, 82
reactance, 93–6, 105–6
recycling, 101
Red Cross, 116, 117
Regional Assistance Mission to the Solomon Islands (RAMSI), 75
Registered Association of Rag-pickers, 100
relationship building, in aid work, 88
research, as power, 24–6
Rhodes, C., 139
Rocha Menochal, A., 111
Rodney, W., 18
Rogerson, A., 111

Sachs, Jeffrey, 1, 10, 141
salaries *see* aid workers, salaries of
Schein, V., 84–5
Schön, C., 126
Schumacher, E. F., 3, 15
Scottish tartan, revival of, 93
Segal, Ronald, 17
Selmer technique, 77
Sen, Amartya, 10, 16, 120–1, 153; *Development as Freedom*, 88, 152; *The Idea of Justice*, 120

Sen, Gita, 23, 149–50
Senghor, Leopold, 16
Shovelin, Michael J., 2
Singapore, migrants in, 51
Singapore Management University, 146
Singer, Peter, *The Life You Can Save*, 100
Slim, H., 116
'small is beautiful', 15
social dominance theory, 22–3, 27, 29, 48, 53, 55, 57, 58; self-reflexive, 26
social enterprise, 148
socialization, 53–4
Solomon Islands, research in, 75–6
South Commission, Report of, 7
Spence, Michael, 14–15
stereotype threat, 92
Stokes, Niall, 40
Stone, Sharon, 39

Tanzania: health workers in, 124 (study of, 68)
technology, maintenance of, 145
Terror Management Theory, 82
theory, new, development of, 24
Tobias, P., 108
traditional healers, undermining of, 142
Transparency International, 35–6
trauma counselling, 85–6
Tsunami, Asian, 127, 136; inter-agency competition in, 128–9

U'wa indigenous group (Colombia), 81, 83
Uganda, 78; Poverty Eradication Action Plan, 37
uMunthu, concept of, 83–4, 99

unbranding, 114
underdevelopment, notion of, 29–30
unfairness, in workplace, 60
unfreezing and refreezing, concept of, 144, 146
United Nations (UN), 17, 47, 52, 116, 117; First Development Decade, 19; seen as gravy train, 54
UN Children's Fund (UNICEF), 116
UN Convention against Corruption, 36
UN Development Programme (UNDP), 98
UN Security Council, 46–7
USAID, 115

vaccines, storage of, 148
Vestergaard, A., 115

Wainaina, Binyavanga, 1
Walpole, S., 24
'wantok' system, 63
Ward, C., 51
Werker, Eric, 107, 108, 109, 112–13
Wheatley, M., 119
Wheeler, Graeme, 15
Whittle, D., 119
Wilkinson, R., 59
women, 102; self-organization of, 101
World Bank, 17, 19, 35, 37, 60, 108, 146
World Health Organization (WHO), 59–60
World Improvement Alliance (WIA), 13–14
World Vision, 107, 127

Yunus, Muhammad, 16, 146–7